The Fellowship of His Sufferings

The Fellowship of His Sufferings

Thoughts and Reflections on the Coptic Orthodox Holy Week

Dr. Hani Ashamalla

Copyright © 2017 **Dr. Hani Ashamalla**
All rights reserved.

ISBN-13: 9781542391412
ISBN-10: 1542391415
Library of Congress Control Number: 2017900373
CreateSpace Independent Publishing Platform
North Charleston, South Carolina

Introduction

In the Orthodox Church, the Great Lent is followed by the Holy Week—or the "Passion Week"—which ends with the Feast of Resurrection. This week is called, among many other names, the Pascha Week. The Jewish Passover, celebrated on Holy Friday, is also called *Pascha*. Like the Coptic Church, all orthodox churches have their own amazing prayers and hymns. The Passion Week is a wonderful week, with beautiful and meaningful melodies that help to stimulate our senses to the life the church is trying to help us live.

These melodies are not the goal in themselves. Thus, participating in these hymns without truly reliving the sufferings of our Lord results in loss of the principal goal of this week. We become like a bride who immensely admires the garment of her groom and forgets the real person she will be marrying.

Many books have been published to help understand these events and rituals. I tried, in this book, to focus on the spiritual meanings and reflections rather than just explaining the texts or the events. That is why you will find a prayer or a meditation following an event or a day of the week. While I am using the rituals practiced during the Coptic Church Passion Week, I expect that non-Coptic readers may still benefit from reading and reflecting on the events. I also dedicated a whole chapter to analyzing the various theories explaining Christ's agony, sufferings, and causes of death from a medical perspective. I tried to use my own background as a medical doctor to help the reader reach a meaningful understanding of the most important event in history—Christ's death.

It is my profound desire that this book will have a transformational impact on how we pray during the Passion Week.

I am indebted to Mrs. Lilian Ghaly for her thorough review and edit of the book. I deeply appreciate the amazing talents of my friends Yasser Abdelmalek in designing the book cover and Remon Hanna in creating the timeline and the map. I am also grateful for the encouragement and the significant additions by His Grace Bishop David, Bishop of New York and New England.

Hani Ashamalla, MD
Deacon at Saint Mary and Saint Antonios Coptic Orthodox Church
Queens, New York

Biblical References

The New King James Version (NKJV) of the Bible is used for all the verses quoted in this book.

Contents

Introduction.. v
Biblical References... vii

The Passover 1
How to Benefit from the Passion Week 5
The Grain of Wheat... 12
Lazarus Saturday 16
Palm Sunday and the Public Funeral 19
The Passion Week 24
Holy Monday.. 25
Holy Tuesday.. 28
Holy Wednesday 32
Holy Thursday.. 37
Passover Dinner 43
The Eve of Friday.. 50
The Trials of Jesus Christ....................................... 57
Holy Friday 65
Christ's Timeline from Arrest to Burial 90
The Lord's Sufferings and Death from a Medical Perspective.... 91

Bibliography·· 105
Symbolic Theatrical Plays ······································ 107
About the Author ·· 139

The Passover

For God so loved the world that He gave His only begotten Son, that whoever believes in Him should not perish but have everlasting life.

—John 3:16

God loved us from the very beginning, even with the foreknowledge that we will sin and deserve condemnation and death. Therefore, He prepared for us a great plan of salvation by sending His only begotten Son, who was incarnated and became man, to carry our sins and perfect our salvation.

The Lord revealed His plan of salvation to His prophets and His people in the book of Exodus. He commanded Moses to tell the people to offer the annual Passover lamb as a sacrifice to cover up their sins:

> Now the Lord spoke to Moses and Aaron in the land of Egypt, saying, "This month shall be your beginning of months; it shall be the first month of the year to you. Speak to all the

congregation of Israel, saying: 'On the tenth of this month every man shall take for himself a lamb, according to the house of his father, a lamb for a household. And if the household is too small for the lamb, let him and his neighbor next to his house take it according to the number of the persons; according to each man's need you shall make your count for the lamb. Your lamb shall be without blemish, a male of the first year. You may take it from the sheep or from the goats. Now you shall keep it until the fourteenth day of the same month. Then the whole assembly of the congregation of Israel shall kill it at twilight. And they shall take some of the blood and put it on the two doorposts and on the lintel of the houses where they eat it. Then they shall eat the flesh on that night; roasted in fire, with unleavened bread and with bitter herbs they shall eat it. Do not eat it raw, nor boiled at all with water, but roasted in fire—its head with its legs and its entrails. You shall let none of it remain until morning, and what remains of it until morning you shall burn with fire. And thus you shall eat it: with a belt on your waist, your sandals on your feet, and your staff in your hand. So you shall eat it in haste. It is the Lord's Passover.

'For I will pass through the land of Egypt on that night, and will strike all the firstborn in the land of Egypt, both man and beast; and against all the gods of Egypt I will execute judgment: I am the Lord. Now the blood shall be a sign for you on the houses where you are. And when I see the blood, I will pass over you; and the plague shall not be on you to destroy you when I strike the land of Egypt.

'So this day shall be to you a memorial; and you shall keep it as a feast to the Lord throughout your generations. You shall keep it as a feast by an everlasting ordinance." (Exod. 12:1–14)

The Israelites, during their suffering in Egypt, cried out to God to save them and remove them from slavery. Thus the Lord spoke to Moses to lead His people to the land flowing with milk and honey—the land of Canaan. However, Pharaoh refused to let the Israelites out of Egypt, so the Lord decided to strike the firstborn of each Egyptian household. In order for God to save the firstborn children of the Israelites who were living together with the Egyptians, He commanded Moses to have each household sacrifice a *Passover lamb* and smear the blood on the two doorposts and on the lintel of the houses. The angel of death, seeing the blood, would then pass over the house.

The Passover lamb is a symbol and a sign of Christ. God wanted to direct the minds of the people to the idea of redemption so that when the Christ comes as the Savior, they would accept Him. Therefore, Passover represents the crucifixion and redemption. Death will pass over those who are sheltered by the blood of Christ—the true Lamb.

Passover was a means of salvation over death, but for the Christians, Christ's death is our salvation.

How to Eat the Passover Lamb

1. "Eat the flesh on that night roasted in fire"*:* This is a reference to the excruciating pain that Christ endured.
2. "With bitter herbs": Christ tasted gall on the cross.
3. "Do not eat it raw or boiled with water, but roasted in fire": The pain that Jesus Christ experienced was real and not imaginary.
4. "You shall let none of it remain until morning": Christ did not stay on the cross long after His death, and they hastily buried Him.

5. "With a belt on your waist, your sandals on your feet, and your staff in your hand": This is evidence of readiness and vigilance.
6. "Without blemish": This is like Christ, who is the lamb without defect.
7. "The whole assembly shall kill it": This is similar to the entire nation of Israel that gathered to kill Christ.
8. "Its head with its legs and its entrails. You shall let none of it remain until morning": Christ suffered from his head to his legs, and He did not remain on the cross till the next day since it was the Sabbath.
9. "Shall kill it at twilight": Our Lord died on the ninth hour and was buried at the twelfth hour—twilight.
10. "Now you shall keep it until the fourteenth day of the same month": Our Lord entered Jerusalem like a lamb on the tenth of the month and was slaughtered like a lamb on the fourteenth of the month.

The Passover lamb is seen as a symbol or the foreshadow of Christ the Savior, who is the original sacrifice. The Jews only saw the symbol and did not comprehend the original. As for us, we saw the original and realized that the Passover lamb was just a symbol.

How to Benefit from the Passion Week

Consecrate a fast, call a sacred assembly.

—Joel 1:14

Christians celebrate the Passion Week on a yearly basis regardless of their denomination; however, the benefits of this week vary depending on the focus and attitude of each person. Some enter the week with no preparedness, and for them, it is an ordinary week like the ones before or after; I doubt that the week will transform them. On the other hand, there are ways to prepare for the Passion Week, and by that we will benefit immensely. If we properly prepare ourselves, the chances of this week transforming us are enhanced.

1. Share in the fellowship of His sufferings (put yourself in the events):
There is a big difference between reading the events from biblical texts and actually living them. Try to envision the events; place yourself in every location. Imagine yourself as a real character in these events, for example:

On Palm Sunday: You are one of the children who is praising saying Hosanna. What did you see? What did you hear? How did Christ look as He entered Jerusalem? Or perhaps you were one of the merchants in the temple, buying and selling when Jesus cast them (and you) out! Did you repent so He may allow you back?

On Thursday: You are Peter. Christ warned you, "You will deny Me!" You said, "Lord, you are mistaken; I will never do it!" But actually, you did; you have denied Christ many times. Did you repent so He may wash your feet?

Perhaps, you are Judas; Christ is about to wash your feet while you are about to betray Him! What should you be feeling in this very sensitive situation?

On Friday: Perhaps you are Barabbas! You were already condemned to death because of your crimes, but at the last hour, you were replaced! Christ took your position and accepted condemnation on your behalf. How would you now feel?

2. Live in true repentance:

Let us be frank with each other; there isn't much you can offer to Christ during His sufferings. You cannot alleviate His pains, nor can you be crucified on His behalf. The only act that Christ will be so thrilled to receive in the midst of His agony is *repentance*. Repentance is the true cup of water you can offer Christ to quench His thirst when He said "I thirst."

Repentance means a change of your ways. In the original meaning of the Greek word *Metanoia* "μετάνοια is "a transformative change of heart or change of direction." That is why the orthodox manner of *Metanoia* is to bow down to the ground and then rise up again. This denotes that with our sins we were brought down to the ground, and through repentance and the grace of God, we rise again.

To benefit from this week, work hard to drop a habit or a sin that you are fighting with. Change your ways by the renewal of the mind (Rom. 12:2).

3. Follow the prayers and readings of the Passion Week:
Regardless of your denomination, if you want to benefit from this amazing week and rejoice in His resurrection, follow the readings of your church. At the very least, read the last few chapters of the four Gospels and parts of the Old Testament (e.g., Isa. 40–63, Ps. 22). Moreover, persist in praying, especially in asking for forgiveness.

4. Reduce your use of social media:
The use of social media is becoming a major competition to Christ. This week belongs only to Christ; if you want to benefit, make a real effort to reduce the time you spend on social media. Imagine that Christ is hanging before your eyes on the cross and you are busy posting in your social accounts!

While fasting is customary in the Orthodox churches before and during the Passion Week, I dare to say that true fasting could be exactly that; fast from the overuse of social media.

5. Do acts of mercy:
Everyone who is need of an act of mercy is actually *Christ in disguise*. "Inasmuch as you did it to one of the least of My brethren, you did it to Me" (Matt. 25:40).

While acts of mercy are desirable to be done at all times, they are considered like the anointing of Jesus's body in the Passion Week. Be Christ to those around you, who may be the Samaritan woman, the paralyzed man, or the blind man. "For to you it has been granted on behalf of Christ, not only to believe in Him but to suffer for His sake" (Phil. 1:29).

To benefit fully from the Passion Week, increase your acts of mercy to anyone—the sick, the poor, the stranger, the reject, and so on.

6. Attend church prayers:
To benefit from the Passion Week, you need to exchange going to some of the places that you normally visit during the week with attending church prayers or Bible-fellowship meetings.

Imagine that Christ is about to wash the feet of everyone, but you decided to go to a unimportant location!

In this week, you need to be under His feet, whether at home or in a place of worship. Mary Magdalene was an amazing character who could not be anywhere except under the feet of His cross.

7. Stay in a state of joy and avoid grumpiness:
Grumpiness is becoming our normal state of everyday attitude. To benefit from the Passion Week, try to be thankful and avoid being grumpy. There are lots of reasons to be grateful, but specifically during this week we should be grateful for the salvation Christ has given us through the cross.

Pascha
The term *Pascha* is a Hebrew word meaning "Passover." The original Jewish word is *Psaah* and in the Coptic or Greek languages, it is πάσχα.

General Ideas Regarding the Holy Week
During the Holy Week, the church does not follow regular time. Rather, it uses Jewish time. The Jewish day starts at sunset at about 6:00 p.m. to sunset the next day.

THE FELLOWSHIP OF HIS SUFFERINGS

For example, Monday begins with the eve of Monday (Sunday after 6:00 p.m.) and ends at 6:00 p.m. on Monday. We can further break it up into the eve of Monday, which is from Sunday 6:00 p.m. to 6:00 a.m. on Monday, and the daytime of Monday, which begins at 6:00 a.m. and ends at 6:00 p.m. on Monday. Then the eve of Tuesday starts, and so on.

1. During **this week**, the altar remains closed, and the church prayers take place outside the altar for the following reasons:
    A. Christ's crucifixion was outside Jerusalem. It is known that the place of crucifixion (Golgotha) is on the outskirts of Jerusalem. Saint Paul wrote, "Therefore Jesus also, that He might sanctify the people with His own blood, suffered outside the gate. Therefore let us go forth to Him, outside the camp, bearing His reproach (Heb. 13:12–13)." Jerusalem is the altar. Hence, we pray outside.
    B. There is no reconciliation between heaven and earth yet. Until this time, God the Father had withheld his face from mankind.
    I hate, I despise your feast days,
    And I do not savor your sacred assemblies.
    Though you offer Me burnt offerings and your grain offerings,
    I will not accept them,
    Nor will I regard your fattened peace offerings.
    Take away from Me the noise of your songs,
    For I will not hear the melody of your stringed instruments. (Amos 5:21–23)

In order to remind ourselves of our former state before Christ's crucifixion and reconciliation, the veil of the altar remains closed. The veil represents the separation between God and man, which is ripped into two pieces on the eleventh hour of Holy Friday after the death of Christ on the cross.

2. There are no liturgies (with the exception of Maundy Thursday Liturgy). This is because the liturgy itself is a form reconciliation. It is a communion between God and man. However, at this time this reconciliation had not yet occurred, since Christ had not yet died on the cross. Furthermore, liturgy consists of a sacrifice, but God at this time was not accepting our sacrifices.
   Bring no more futile sacrifices;
   Incense is an abomination to Me.
   The New Moons, the Sabbaths, and the calling of assemblies—
   I cannot endure iniquity and the sacred meeting.
   Your New Moons and your appointed feasts
   My soul hates;
   They are a trouble to Me,
   I am weary of bearing them.
   When you spread out your hands,
   I will hide My eyes from you;
   Even though you make many prayers,
   I will not hear.
   Your hands are full of blood. (Isa. 1:13–15)
3. There's no use of incense, with the exception of Maundy Thursday. Incense indicates again that there is reconciliation: "Let my prayer be set before You as incense, the lifting up of my hands as the evening sacrifice." (Ps. 141:2)
4. There's no *Agpeya* (Prayer Book of the Hours). The *Agpeya* consists of Psalms, which contain many prophecies other than

those on the crucifixion. For example, the incarnation, the life of Christ, and the resurrection are all prophesied about in the Psalms. During the Holy Week, the church's sole focus is on the crucifixion. Therefore, the church uses the Psalms about the crucifixion but does not use the Agpeya as a whole; in addition, the church replaces the Psalms with the praise "to Thine is the power" twelve times per hour.

The Grain of Wheat

Most assuredly, I say to you, unless a grain of wheat falls into the ground and dies, it remains alone; but if it dies, it produces much grain. He who loves his life will lose it, and he who hates his life in this world will keep it for eternal life.

—John 12:24

The "grain of wheat" is very clearly associated with the Passion Week. The Lord Jesus Christ uses the parable of the grain of wheat that needed to fall on the ground and be buried under soil to produce fruits. This parable is read by the church at the beginning of Pascha on the eve of Monday. We are able to follow this grain of wheat each day until it is buried on Friday through the readings, which are guided by the Holy Spirit.

Pascha Week begins right after Palm Sunday when Christ entered into Jerusalem.

The Order of Prayers

The church prays five prayers in the morning, which are called morning Pascha prayers, and five evening prayers, which are called evening Pascha prayers. The five prayers are as follows:

First Hour:	This correlates to 6:00 a.m. for the morning Pascha and 6:00 p.m. for the evening Pascha.
Third Hour:	This correlates to 9:00 a.m. for the morning Pascha and 9:00 p.m. for the evening Pascha.
Sixth Hour:	This correlates to twelve noon for the morning Pascha and twelve midnight for the evening Pascha.
Ninth Hour:	This correlates to 3:00 p.m. for the morning Pascha and 3:00 a.m. for the evening Pascha.
Eleventh Hour:	This correlates to 5:00 p.m. for the morning Pascha and 5:00 a.m. for the evening Pascha.
Twelfth Hour:	This is prayed only on Good Friday and represents the burial of our Savior, which translates to 6:00 p.m.

Note: You can figure out the correlating time by adding six to the hour number. For example, for the third hour, add three and six, and you get 9:00 a.m. and 9:00 p.m.

Each hour consists of the following:

A. Prophecies are collected from Old Testament books to coincide with the events of the hour or the day.
B. Praises: "Thine is the power, the glory, the blessing, the majesty" is chanted twelve times, alternating between the two

sides of the congregation. This replaces the twelve Psalms per hour of the *Agpeya* during the Holy Week. This hymn is taken from the praises of the angels in heaven.

> And I looked, and I heard the voice of many angels around the throne and the animals and the elders, and their number was myriads of myriads and thousands of thousands, saying with a loud voice, "Worthy is the Lamb that was slain to receive power and wealth and wisdom and strength and honor and glory and blessing." And every creature which is in heaven and on earth and under the earth, and the sea, all that is in them, I heard saying: for sitting on the throne and to the Lamb blessing and honor and glory and dominion forever and ever. (Rev. 5:11–13)

The Church reminds us that Jesus was not crucified in weakness but out of love—for our salvation.

> Since you seek a proof of Christ speaking in me, who is not weak toward you, but mighty in you. For though He was crucified in weakness, yet He lives by the power of God. For we also are weak in Him, but we shall live with Him by the power of God toward you. (2 Cor. 13:3–4)

We chant "my Lord Jesus Christ" each hour until the eleventh hour of Tuesday. We then add "my Lord Jesus Christ, my Good Savior" before reading the Gospel of the Eleventh Hour: "He said to his disciples, 'After two days is the Passover, and the Son of Man is betrayed to be crucified'" (Matt. 26: 2). The church is like a faithful bride when she sees her groom suffering for her; she calls Him "my Good

Savior," as the Apostle Paul said, "who loved me and gave Himself for me" (Gal. 2:20).

On the eve of Friday (Thursday evening), the Church witnesses Christ arrested and everyone abandoning Him, so we add the phrase "my salvation and my song and has become to me a Sacred salvation" (Ps. 118:14).

- C. The Psalm is chanted in a sad tune called the *Edrybi* tune.
- D. The Gospel shows the highlighted events of that hour.
- E. The exposition is given—an interpretation of the events of the Bible.
- F. Litanies: There are morning and evening prayers, each followed by "Lord, have mercy."

Lazarus Saturday

Now Jesus loved Martha and her sister and Lazarus. So, when He heard that he was sick, He stayed two more days in the place where He was.

—John 11:5–6

Lazarus Saturday is the Saturday before the Passion Week. It is considered to be the link between Lent and the Holy Week, the link between life and death. The Jewish Sabbath is celebrated as the day that God rested. Although God rested from creating, He continued to maintain and care for His creation.

After the Lord's resurrection, the Church began to regard Sunday as the day of the Lord. Hence, the Saturday of Lazarus is the last Sabbath.

On this Saturday, the Lord raised Lazarus from the dead—after Lazarus had been dead for four days. This miracle became a major cause of jealousy among the Jews toward Jesus Christ. The Jews began to mastermind the plot to arrest Him, as the miracle had gained great resonance with many people. Many of them had visited the house of Mary and Martha to sympathize with the death of their brother. A few days later, they found themselves back to celebrate Lazarus's resurrection from the dead. The next day (Sunday), Lazarus and the Lord entered Jerusalem together, and this caused the Jews to plot to kill Lazarus, too.

> Now a great many of the Jews knew that He was there; and they came, not for Jesus's sake only, but that they might also see Lazarus, whom He had raised from the dead. But the chief priests plotted to put Lazarus to death also, because on account of him many of the Jews went away and believed in Jesus. (John 12:9–11)

Mary and Martha hosted a big party on the night of Palm Sunday to celebrate the miracle of their brother coming back to life.

Meditation

When God Is Delayed

Mary and Martha (Lazarus's sisters) sent for You, pleading to save their brother and saying, "Lord, behold, he whom You love is sick." But You stayed where You were two more days.

My Lord, I understand now Your wisdom when I call upon you while in tribulation, and You take Your time.

I used to think You never listened to my pleas or You don't love me. How wrong I was, yet You have heard me from the first cry.

Your response is timed by Your Wisdom and not timed by my need.

Your response may come even after I have lost all hope and everything sounds depressing. This is the point You come in. You come to give resurrection as You had done for Lazarus.

Now I understand, and when I see You delayed, I will know that You are intending a great work at the level of raising Lazarus from the dead.

If You had come when Lazarus was sick, the miracle would not have been so great. Instead, You waited for days.

How great is Your delay, O Lord! I will wait for You always.

Palm Sunday and the Public Funeral

Palm Sunday is one of the seven major feasts of our Lord. The celebration of Palm Sunday is the only celebration that our Lord not only accepted but He even planned to be greeted as a king.

It is estimated that half a million people greeted Jesus Christ that day, and He was pleased to have their praises. Before that day, He generally never accepted the praise offered to Him as a king.

The whole town shook from the cries and the praises of the multitude who cried out, saying, "Hosanna, Hosanna in the highest." This is the only major feast where all four gospels are read in the Orthodox tradition.

The Hebrew word *Hosanna* (or *Yashoaana*) comes from two components: "Yasha," which means "save us," and "Anna," which means "we implore you." Hence, Hosanna means "We implore You to save us."

Jesus Christ entered Jerusalem, and the first thing he did was to enter into "His house" or into Solomon's temple.

This is the most important site in all Jerusalem. When He entered, he was greeted by a scene that made Him, for the first and only time, "angry."

The high priests had been renting the outer yard to the merchants of pigeons, sheep, cows, and so on, in addition to the money-exchange booths. The house of God appeared like a flea market; hence, He said, "My house shall be called a house of prayer, but you have made it a 'den of thieves'" (Matt. 21:13).

He made a whip of cords and drove all those merchants away: "When He had made a whip of cords, He drove them all out of the temple, with the sheep and the oxen, and poured out the changers' money and overturned the tables" (John 2:15).

Prayer
"My House, Not Your House"

Lord, if I am hiding any sin in my heart, I am ready to receive Your whip of cords on my back, but do not leave my heart (*Your house*) to be desolate and become a house of thieves.

He had made a whip of cords; He drove them all out of the temple with the sheep and the oxen and poured out the changers' money and overturned the tables.

Lord, I want You to enter my heart as You had entered Jerusalem.

Lord, I want You to enter as a king into my heart, and no other king should have my throne.

Lord, I want You to overturn the merchants' tables in my life.

Lord, I want You to drive out all that is not suitable for Your house.

Lord, don't say, "*Your house is left to you desolate*" (Matt. 23:38). Lord, say, "Your house is going to be My house—a house of prayer."

Lord, "enter and stay in Your resting place" (Psalm 132:8).

Lord, will You enter into my Jerusalem (my heart)? Or have You found another king on my throne?

Lord, I am worried that I praise You with palms today and few days later I lift you on the cross.

Lord, have mercy on me.

Lord, I implore You to save me.

Lord, Hosanna!

The Public Funeral Prayer

The Coptic Orthodox Church prays a public funeral prayer immediately after the Palm Sunday prayers. In the past, this prayer used to be performed a few hours after the Palm Sunday liturgy, but in order to take into consideration the distance that many people travel, the prayer now follows the actual feast liturgy.

The concept of this prayer is to allow the entire congregation to attend their own "funeral prayer." Should anyone die during the Passion Week, the church will not perform a formal funeral prayer. Rather, the departed and the family attend a Pascha prayer before burial. The reason behind this concept is that the church is solely focused on the death of Christ this week.

Meditation

"When I Attended My Own Funeral!"

Lord, You made me attend and listen to with my own ears my own funeral!

Lord, it would not matter at all if they chanted certain songs or not, if they said good words about me or not, or if a certain person attended the prayers or not.

These issues may have been important to me but will never matter on the day of my funeral.

Only one question will matter. One question will be important to me!

Lord, will you be pleased with me on the day of my funeral…or not?

Lord, have mercy on me!

The Passion Week

The jealousy the high priests felt had reached its maximum by the Passion Week. Thousands of people were following Christ. He had entered the temple and threatened the existence of the high priests by claiming that they had made the house of God a den of thieves. The Pharisees began to say among themselves, "You see that you are accomplishing nothing. Look, the world has gone after Him!" (John 12:19).

So they began their search for a person to betray the Lord.

Holy Monday

Inasmuch as these people draw near with their mouths
and honor Me with their lips,
But have removed their hearts far from Me.

—Isaiah 29:13

Holy Monday starts from 6:00 p.m. on Sunday evening until 6:00 p.m. on Monday.

The sufferings of our Lord began when he entered Jerusalem.

He entered Jerusalem as a Passover lamb on the tenth of Nissan, hailed by thousands of people. He stayed in Jerusalem until the Passover on the fourteenth of Nissan, which is the day when the Passover lamb is slaughtered and eaten.

On each of these five days, like any Passover lamb, He would be examined ever so closely to find out if He showed any defects, in which case He may be rejected.

Our Lord Jesus Christ was examined by the high priests and Pharisees on a daily basis to find a defect in Him. Because he was found without guilt or defect, He would be offered as a sacrifice.

On Monday, our Lord fasted. He saw from afar a fig tree full of leaves, as if it had a lot of fruits. He went seeking fruits but found none, only leaves.

The Lord cursed the tree, saying, "Let no one eat fruit from you ever again" (Mark 11:14), and it withered immediately.

On the next day (Tuesday), when they passed by the tree, they found it withered. They said, "Rabbi, look! The fig tree which You cursed has withered away" (Mark 11:21).Some may ask, "What sin did the tree commit? Why would Christ curse a tree?" The truth is that the Lord cursed the tree for two reasons.

1. He was judging the Jewish nation.
The Jewish nation had a beautiful image, magnificent temple, amazing priestly attire, lovely hymns, and music in their prayers, but their hearts were far away from God. They were lacking faith, love, and obedience to the commandments: "These people draw near to Me with their mouth, and honor Me with their lips, but their heart is far from Me" (Matt. 15:8).

2. He was cursing hypocrisy.
Adam tried to cover his sin with fig leaves, without repenting or confessing his actions (Gen. 3:7). He thought that the fig leaves would cover him well and that there would be no need for repentance. This saddened God's heart immensely; God desired that Adam would confess his transgression and God would cover him with His blood rather than these unsuccessful attempts made by Adam.

God curses the outer beautiful image when He finds no fruits. God wants us to reveal our defects and weaknesses before Him, so He may cleanse and cover us with His blood. But if we insist on showing off our false outer beauty, He will say, "I will vomit you out of My mouth, Because you say, 'I am rich, have become wealthy, and have need of nothing'—and do not know that you are wretched, miserable, poor, blind, and naked" (Rev. 3:17).

Meditation
"Let Me Uncover My Fakeness"

Lord, I know how much You hated the fig leaves. These leaves did not let Adam and Eve repent and confess their transgressions.

So you cast them out of paradise.

Lord, these are the same leaves that make me look righteous in my own eyes.

These are the same leaves that make me look beautiful in the eyes of others.

But I know I cannot hide from your eyes: "Your eyes penetrate the darkness, Your eyes like a flame of fire" (Rev. 2:18). Your eyes see openly what is covered by the fig leaves.

Lord, let me uncover my nakedness, my poverty, and my wretchedness.

You are capable of covering me up, not with useless leaves but by Your grace.

Lord, You were willing to accept the worst of the sinners and forgave them.

But You judged the hypocrites—those dressed in leaves.

Lord, help me take off this attire of fakeness, one leaf at a time.

Help me to approach You *as I am*, and put on me the dress of Your righteousness rather than the leaves of hypocrisy.

Have mercy on me!

Holy Tuesday

Let us be glad and rejoice and give Him glory, for the marriage of the Lamb has come, and His wife has made herself ready.

—Revelation 19:7

The Lord passed by the fig tree and found it had withered. The disciples also noted the change.

He spent that day in Enya's house, which literally means "house of tribulations."

The Lord spoke many parables that day: many related to the end of the world, and some related to the parables of the wedding.

The Passion Week is a journey that ends with our wedding; our groom is preparing to give His bride His best jewelry: "the cross."

An example of the parable relating to the end of days was the parable of the keeper of a vineyard who wanted to cut a tree: "Cut it down; why does it use up the ground?" (Luke 13:7). But Christ interceded, saying: "Lord, let it alone this year also, till I shall dig about it and dung it" (Luke 13:8), which coincides with the last year that our Lord is going to serve in the flesh.

The "wicked vinedressers" is another parable that is also read on Tuesday of the Passion Week. This parable has an amazing concordance to the events of this week. God sent prophets and messengers, but the Jews insulted some and killed the others. At the end of the day, He sent His only begotten son, but they insulted Him, tortured Him, and then killed Him: "But those vinedressers said among themselves, 'This is the heir. Come, let us kill him, and the inheritance will be ours.' 8 So they took him and killed him and cast him out of the vineyard." (Mark 12:7-8).

The Parables of the Wedding
The Ten Virgins (Matt. 25:1-13):
The ten virgins are all similar from the outside. They are all virgins, have lamps, and fall asleep when the groom is delayed. But the most apparent difference is the lack of oil in the foolish virgins' lamps. This is the work of the Holy Spirit in the daily life of the believer—each one needs to collect one drop of oil each day through prayers, services, and love to others so that he or she may stand before the just Judge with no condemnation. They were told, "Go rather to those who sell, and buy for yourselves" (Matt. 25:9). Those who sell are the poor, the needy, and the afflicted, among others. This parable also reminds us to be prepared for the second coming.

The Wedding of the Son of the King (Matt. 22:1-14):
This parable depicts how God prepares for us a table so that we may eat with Him even though none is deserving! Everyone was cleansed and was given a free wedding garment, which resembled the garment of Baptism, at the entrance to the festivity. When the king came down to see the guests, he found one with no wedding garment. In other words, he never entered through the door, which is Christ: "I

am the door of the sheep" (John 10:7). Since he never put on the baptismal garment, the king cast him out, saying, "Friend, how did you come in here without a wedding garment?" (Matt. 22:12). We ought to remind ourselves to have our wedding garment be always ready through renewing our baptism by continual repentance. Christ is the "door", whoever does not enter through the true door is a thief *"I am the door. If anyone enters by Me, he will be saved, and will go in and out and find pasture* (John 10: 9). Those who entered through the door; baptized and repenting are the ones who are sharing in the wedding of the king's son.

Meditation

"Until When Would I Decline Your Invite?"

Until when are You going to invite me to your royal table and I decline?

Until when are You going to prepare the table for us to dine together and I decline?

Until when are You going to ask me to stay up for one hour and I decline?

Until when are You going to ask me to be your faithful bride and I decline?

Until when are You going to ask me not to let go of my wedding garment and I decline?

Until when are You going to ask me to collect oil in my lamp and I decline?

Until when are You going to stay ready, waiting to come and I decline?

Until when are You going to wait for me to produce fruits and I decline?

Lord, don't say, "Cut it down." Leave it alone this year.

Lord, have mercy on me!

Holy Wednesday

Your tongue devises destruction,
Like a sharp razor, working deceitfully. You love evil
more than good,
Lying rather than speaking righteousness.
You love all devouring words, you deceitful tongue.

—Psalm 52:2–4

Two important events occurred on this day. The woman who poured the ointment on Jesus' feet and Judas' betrayal.

1. A woman poured ointment on Jesus's body.
This woman is different from Mary, Lazarus's sister, who had poured ointment on Jesus's feet on Saturday. The aroma of the ointment symbolizes the sweet aroma of the cross, which pleased God, so He forgave us our sins. When she poured the perfume, the following happened:

   a. The disciples (especially Judas) complained about the wasted money: "This he said, not that he cared for the poor, but because he was a thief, and had the money box; and he used to take what was put in it" (John 12:6). Judas was quite annoyed by this act: "'For it might have been sold for more than three hundred denarii and given to the poor.' And they criticized her sharply" *(Mark 14:5).* He was annoyed because he felt it was wasteful to be used on Christ. Christ said this action would be told to the whole world.

  b. Judas betrayed Christ. The value of our Lord in Judas's eyes became so low that he was ready to *sell* Him at any price. Hence, he agreed to sell our Lord for the price of a slave, or "thirty pieces of silver." According to Exodus 21:32, "If the ox gores a male or female servant, he shall give to their master thirty shekels of silver, and the ox shall be stoned." Strangely, Judas would have gotten more if he had asked for more, but when his master's value had become so low, any price was a good price since he only cared to get some money.

More than likely, there are several women who would have poured ointment on Jesus's body.

Here are other similar events:

1. On Wednesday of the Passion Week, while Jesus was in Bethany in the home of Simon the leper, the sinful woman poured ointment on Jesus's feet. This woman's name is not mentioned (Mark 14:3, Matt. 26:6).
2. On Saturday (Lazarus's Saturday), Mary (Lazarus's sister) poured ointment on Jesus's feet when he was in Lazarus's house after Lazarus was raised from the dead (John 12).
3. Before the Passion Week (unknown timing), another sinful woman—some think it was Mary Magdalene—poured ointment on Jesus's feet in the Pharisee's house (Luke 7:36-50).

2- Judas Iscariot betraying our Lord:

There is a clear opposition between love and betrayal. On the same day, the sinful woman poured the perfume and the disciple betrayed his master. The woman bought perfume to pour on Jesus's feet with three hundred denarii (equivalent a year's wage today, possibly $30,000) (Mark Allan Powell, 2009), while the disciple sold Jesus for thirty pieces of silver. This unit of silver was equal to 6,000 Greek drachmae or Roman denarii (equivalent to about $300 today). The disciple, Judas, had been in close proximity to Christ. He'd witnessed Christ's love, His miracles, and His teachings. However, Judas's love of money was stronger than anything he had witnessed during his time with Christ.

Meditation
Friend, Why Did You Come?

Am I coming to bring ointment to pour on Jesus's body, or am I bringing betrayal?
Am I coming to praise Christ or to sell Him?

The ointment can be many things but mainly displays the importance of submitting oneself under the feet of Christ. We must break our own pride, like the broken pure nard bottle, in order for the sweet smell to spread and please our Lord.

How much did I sell Christ for?

Did I sell Him for Thirty silver, or even less—with a lust or a desire

Am I coming to offer the nard perfume of my repentance—the nard perfume of my loving service—or am I coming to sell with the dimes of desires and my busy life? And give what is leftover only?

Our Lord will always remember our ointment: *"Assuredly, I say to you, wherever this gospel is preached in the whole world, what this woman has done will also be told as a memorial to her"* (Matt. 26:13). God will never forget your ointment, irrespective of whether it was poured on His head (act of praises) or on His feet (acts of mercy).

Will I sit at Christ's feet and celebrate Him, or will I see Him as a slave?

Prayer

Lord, do I sell you- like Judas- for any cheap price?
    Or I value you as my master and Lord and offer you my best?
    This woman You praised desired you as a Groom, a King, and a Savior, but Judas—"one of the twelve"—sold You for the price of a slave.
Lord, You are being sold today…why did You let Judas price You?
Lord, You came in the form of a man and obeyed even unto death—death on the cross.
Lord, You were in the form of a slave…and now You have agreed to be sold as a slave.
Lord, do I know Your value?
Lord, do I leave the whole world to sit under Your feet?
Lord, have mercy on me!

Holy Thursday

(Also, known as the "Great Thursday" or "Covenant Thursday")

Even my own familiar friend in whom I trusted,
Who ate my bread, has lifted up his heel against me.

—Psalm 41:9

As mentioned before, the sanctuary is closed for the whole week. However, it is opened on Thursday as an exception.

The sanctuary is opened during the first hour of the Thursday of the Holy Pascha, and then it is closed to be opened only during the Liturgy.

In the first hour of Thursday, the prophecies are read, the sanctuary is opened, the doxology or the praise *"Thok te tigom"* is prayed, and the thanksgiving prayer is chanted.

We read the chapter related to Judas's betrayal from the book of Acts: *"Now this man purchased a field with the wages of iniquity; and falling headlong, he burst open in the middle and all his entrails gushed out"* (Acts 1:18).

Then a unique procession is carried out called "Judas's Procession": "Judas…Judas…who has broken the law, with silver you have sold Christ to the Jews, who have broken the law."

The concept of this procession is to judge ourselves while we are chanting and engage in self-examination by wondering the following:

- "Am I selling the Lord as Judas did?"
- "Am I selling Him for my own desires?"
- "Is Christ more precious to me than all the money of the world?"
- "Do I need to reevaluate what's important to me?"

This procession is different from any other church procession done throughout the liturgical year. All other processions throughout the year are performed counterclockwise (going toward the right once it exits the sanctuary), meaning that the church is living "outside worldly time," while Judas's procession goes clockwise (going toward to the left once it exits the sanctuary) because he followed the worldly path.

Once the first hour of the Pascha is completed, the sanctuary is closed again and the third-, sixth-, and ninth-hour prayers are prayed outside the sanctuary.

There are two "main events" that occurred on Thursday:

1. **Washing of the feet:** Our Lord rose from supper, took off His outer garment, girded Himself with a towel, put water in a basin, and began washing the feet of His disciples and wiping them with a towel.
2. **Eucharist:** The Lord established the sacrament of Communion on Covenant Thursday. "This is the bread which the angels desire to watch and they are not allowed…

we are allowed to eat" (inaudible prayers for the priest in St. Basil Liturgy prayers).

In the original Jewish custom, it was the youngest servant or son who washed the *hands* of those about to dine. But what happened during the washing of the feet made all the disciples marvel. The head of the supper was the One who was serving and washing the feet—not even the hands!

The Coptic Orthodox Church resembles her Groom; every Holy Thursday, the highest priesthood present in the church—priest, hegemon, or bishop—washes the feet of the whole congregation.

It is likely that Judas did not participate in the last cup of the last supper, which was the Eucharist. He left after the third cup was passed.

Here's the dialogue between Jesus and Peter:

> Peter could not imagine that our Lord would wash his feet and told Him, "You will not wash my feet."
>
> Peter said to Him, "You shall never wash my feet!" Jesus answered him, "If I do not wash you, you have no part with Me." Simon Peter said to Him, "Lord, not my feet only, but also my hands and my head!" Jesus said to him, "He who is bathed needs only to wash his feet, but is completely clean; and you are clean, but not all of you." For He knew who would betray Him; therefore He said, "You are not all clean." (John 13: 8–11)

Most of the Church fathers agree that Christ was speaking here about Baptism, where you only need to be bathed once but you will need to repent daily, which is depicted here by the "washing of your feet."

Christ continued later to state that He must be crucified and Peter would offer his help. Jesus answered him:

> Where I am going you cannot follow Me now, but you shall follow Me afterward." Peter said to Him, "Lord, why can I not follow You now? I will lay down my life for Your sake." Jesus answered him, "Will you lay down your life for My sake? Most assuredly, I say to you, the rooster shall not crow till you have denied Me three times." (John 13:36–38)

We will see how Peter reacted to these words shortly.

Meditation

You Wash My Feet?

Lord, how great is Your humility…you are at the feet of the church, washing not only those who are worthy but every "Judas" in the congregation.
While I am approaching the priest to have my feet washed, what are my feelings?

Say…
    Lord, you told your disciples, "You are not all clean" (John 13:11). Lord, I am the most unclean in Your congregation, in this church. Lord, cleanse me!

    Lord, I don't want to be "unclean" or "lift my foot" to crush Your hands like Judas: "Even my own familiar friend in whom I trusted, who ate my bread, has lifted up his heel against me" (Psalm 41:9).

    Lord, please wash me thoroughly from all my iniquities and cleanse me from all my sins!

Prayer

"You wash my feet?" Peter said.

"You wash my feet?" I say.

Lord, how can You be at my feet?

Your submission, Your humility…I cannot comprehend them.

Lord, the lady poured perfume on Your feet on Wednesday, breaking her bottle at Your feet.

Lord, I saw You bend down over my feet like a broken perfume bottle.

You are washing my feet?

Lord, You saw the fruitless tree, and You cursed it. What did You see when You washed my feet?

I deserve the curse because I did not produce the fruits You desired.

What did You think when You were washing my feet?

Did You say I deserve the curse?

Lord, I plead to You, give me one more chance!

Lord, let me be the one who washes Your feet.

Let me wash the feet of Your children.

Let me learn to forgive, so I do not deserve the curse!

Lord, have mercy on me!

Passover Dinner

During the Passover, there are four types of cups:

- a cup of thanks for the angel of death, which passed by the doors of the Jews without condemning them;
- a cup of the slaughtered Passover lamb (propitiation);
- a cup of the blessings for the salvation; and
- a cup of praises for the kingdom of God.

It is logical to think that John was sitting, as was his custom, next to the Lord. It is also logical to think that Peter was on the other side of the Lord or across from him, while Judas was in the vicinity of the Lord in order to dip his hand in the pot with Christ:

> Jesus answered, "It is he to whom I shall give a piece of bread when I have dipped it." And having dipped the bread, He gave it to Judas Iscariot, the son of Simon. (John 13:26)
>
> Now after the piece of bread, Satan entered him. Then Jesus said to him, "What you do, do quickly." But no one at the table knew for what reason He said this to him. For some thought, because Judas had the money box, that Jesus had said to him, "Buy those things we need for the feast," or that he should give something to the poor. (John 13:27–29)

It is likely that the rest of the disciples who were seated a little farther away did not hear what Christ said to Judas, while those were close, because of their simple hearts, assumed Judas was good rather than the worst about him. They only realized it too late when they saw Judas in Gethsemane, kissing Jesus as the sign given to the soldiers of the temple to arrest Him.

What Did They Eat on Thursday? Was It the Passover Meal?

There are two opinions:

1. Thursday was the Passover.

Those who hold this opinion depend on this verse: *"Then they led Jesus from Caiaphas to the Praetorium, and it was early morning. But they themselves did not go into the Praetorium, lest they should be defiled, but that they might eat the Passover"* (John 18:28).

They use this verse as evidence that the unleavened feast had started. This feast begins immediately after Passover (the fifteenth of Nissan to the twenty-second of Nissan). This feast conceptualizes the lifting/removal of any fragment of bread that might have fallen in any corner of the house. The head of the house, using a candle or a lamp, will search carefully before the feast begins. Saint Paul modified the Jewish understanding of the feast into a new Christian idea. He writes, *"Therefore let us keep the feast, not with old leaven, nor with the leaven of malice and wickedness, but with the unleavened bread of sincerity and truth"* (1 Cor. 5:8).

Those who contradict this opinion base their opposition on the fact that Christ and His disciples did not eat the Passover lamb on Thursday but rather ate the *Karpas* or the bitter herbs. They explain that this day is what the Eastern people practice up to this day on the night before the wedding, when they have a special meal and they call it *Leilet El-hennah*.

2. Friday is the Passover and the day of slaughtering the lamb. We must differentiate between two events:

- the slaughtering of the lamb, which occurs on the fourteenth of Nissan
- the eating of the Passover lamb, which occurs on the fifteenth of Nissan

The lamb, which was chosen five days ago (on Palm Sunday), will be slaughtered today. This happens during the ninth hour on the fourteenth of Nissan, which is quite in accordance with what occurred on the day that Jesus ate the Passover, exchanging the Jewish Passover with the Eucharist: *"With fervent desire I have desired to eat this Passover with you before I suffer"* (Luke 22:15).

Then our Lord was arrested on the eve of Friday, was crucified, and then died on the ninth hour of Friday, coinciding with the time of eating the lamb: *"For indeed Christ, our Passover, was sacrificed for us"* (1 Cor. 5:7).

The three synoptic gospels agree that our Lord ate the Passover at its usual time (Thursday the fourteenth of Nissan):

- Matthew 26:18–19: And He said, "Go into the city to a certain man, and say to him, 'The Teacher says, "My time is at hand; I will keep the Passover at your house with My disciples."'" So the disciples did as Jesus had directed them; and they prepared the Passover.
- Mark 14:14–15: Wherever he goes in, say to the master of the house, "The Teacher says, 'Where is the guest room in which

I may eat the Passover with My disciples?'" Then he will show you a large upper room, furnished and prepared; there make ready for us.
- Luke 22:7–8: Then came the Day of Unleavened Bread, when the Passover must be killed. And He sent Peter and John, saying, "Go and prepare the Passover for us, that we may eat."

What about the timing of the Passover in the Gospel of John?

- John 18:28: Then they led Jesus from Caiaphas to the Praetorium, and it was early morning. But they themselves did not go into the Praetorium, lest they should be defiled, but that they might eat the Passover.
- John 19:14: Now it was the Preparation Day of the Passover, and about the sixth hour. And he said to the Jews, "Behold your King!"
- John 19:31: Therefore, because it was the Preparation Day, that the bodies should not remain on the cross on the Sabbath (for that Sabbath was a high day), the Jews asked Pilate that their legs might be broken, and that they might be taken away.

Many of the fathers agree that the Jews may have postponed the timing of the Passover until after they had rid themselves of Jesus. They felt that their chance came about when Judas offered his services. This may explain why they could not enter Pilate's house "lest they should be defiled," and why "this Sabbath was a high day," since this Sabbath coincided with the Passover, enhancing its significance.

Josephus wrote that postponing the Passover was not an uncommon occurrence by the chiefs of the Jews. Other church fathers agree with the same concept, like John Chrysostom, Eusebius, Saint Efrem the Syrian, Pope Theophilus (the twenty-third Pope of Alexandria), and others.

Thursday Liturgy

This is the day of establishing the new covenant for the New Testament through His blood, which will be poured on the cross the following day. This is why the church opens the sanctuary for a short liturgy, although the conciliation between heaven and earth—or, rather, between the Heavenly Father and man—has not yet been completed. It is as if the church takes permission to eat His body and drink His blood on the day the sacrament was established.

Hence, this liturgy is different from any other liturgy of the whole year:

- We do not pray the reconciliation prayer; the reconciliatory act has not happened yet.
- There is no commemoration (citing the names of the saints); we are concerned this day with the Only Holy One.
- There is no prayer for the "departed." The church is again concentrating on Christ and his death.
- There is a special "fraction prayer" that is prayed in this liturgy called "Isaac's Fraction," which cites the amazing similarity between Isaac, who is being offered as a sacrifice by his own father, and Christ, who is being offered by God (His Father) as a sacrifice for the whole world.

The Fraction of "Isaac's Slaughtering"

The similarities between Isaac and Christ are as follows:

- Abraham took his beloved and only begotten son to slaughter as an acceptable sacrifice.
- Isaac carried the wood of the offering, and Christ carried the wood of the cross.
- Isaac returned alive, and Christ rose from the dead.

However, there are also important dissimilarities:

- God the Father took upon Himself what He could not impose on Abraham. God the Father had mercy on Abraham and did not let him touch his son. However, He did not have mercy on His own Son and offered Him as a sacrifice for all: *"He who did not spare His own Son, but delivered Him up for us all, how shall He not with Him also freely give us all things?"* (Rom. 8:32).
- Isaac was driven to the slaughter by his loving father, while Christ was dragged to the cross by the cruel Romans and Jews because of their hate and envy.
- Christ was so tormented to see His mother on his way to the cross, while Isaac did not see Sarah, his mother, on his way to the mountain.

Meditation and Prayer

The Food I Give You Is Food Indeed!

Lord, You established a new covenant today, a covenant You designed with Your holy body and holy blood.
You broke Your body with the knife of love before Your body was broken by the cross.
You poured Your blood by the spear of love before Your side was pierced by the soldier.

Lord, You have given me life through Your living body and blood.
You have given me to eat what the angels desire to see.
Help me to be transformed into Your image.

Lord, if man is what he eats, I want to be spiritual because I am eating from the spiritual food that the angels desire to see.
You have offered this food for me while I am a sinner and for that I am so grateful.

Lord, have mercy on me!

The Eve of Friday

What are these wounds between your arms? Then he will answer, "Those with which I was wounded in the house of my friends."

—Zechariah 13:6

This is the longest Pascha of the whole week because the four gospels are read during each hour, citing all the events of that hour as described by each of the evangelists.

After Christ had eaten the Last Supper with His disciples and celebrated the first Eucharist, but before He went to the Garden of Gethsemane, He started to pray his unique intercessory prayer to His Father as written in John 17.

This prayer is considered the most beautiful prayer between Jesus the Son and God the Father. This prayer is commonly called the "Priestly Prayer," as He intercedes as the high priest before God on behalf of the entire world.

After this prayer, they all went to Gethsemane. Jerusalem was usually crowded during this time of the year because of all the Jews who came from all over the world to celebrate Passover. Therefore, the poor disciples could not find any decent place to stay and ended up in the garden. This may explain the reason why the disciples were sleeping when Jesus was praying in Gethsemane.

Jesus took three of His disciples (Peter, John, and James) to pray separately, leaving the rest a little farther away. He pleaded to the Father, saying, *"Father, if it is Your will, take this cup away from Me; nevertheless not My will, but Yours, be done"* (Luke 22:42).

"And being in agony, He prayed more earnestly. Then His sweat became like great drops of blood falling down to the ground" (Luke 22:44). As He was praying, a rare medical condition occurred, which some call "hematohidrosis," (Jerajani et al. 2009)—where during severe stress sweat glands of the skin open up and release drops of blood. This can also be seen in Mark 14:34–36 and Matt. 26:42.

In the first hour of the eve of Friday Pascha prayers, Jesus prayed three times, and after each time, He returned to check on the three who were closest to Him. Each time He found them sleeping.

The first time He prayed, saying, *"Father, if it is Your will, take this cup away from Me; nevertheless not My will, but Yours, be done"* (Luke 22:42). After the second prayer, He returned to them, saying, *"Simon, are you sleeping? Could you not watch one hour? Watch and pray, lest you enter into temptation. The spirit indeed is willing, but the flesh is weak"* (Mark 14:37–38).

After His third prayer, when He found them still asleep, He said, *"Are you still sleeping and resting? It is enough! The hour has come; behold, the Son of Man is being betrayed into the hands of sinners. Rise, let us be going. See, My betrayer is at hand"* (Mark 14:41–42).

Judas arrived and gave a sign to the temple soldiers: *"Whomever I kiss, He is the One; seize Him"* (Matt. 26:48). He used the sign of love as a symbol of betrayal.

Jesus was wounded in the house of His beloved: *"What are these wounds between your arms? Then he will answer, 'Those with which I was wounded in the house of my friends'"* (Zech. 13:6).

At this point, the disciples woke up because of the chaos; Peter drew his sword and struck the high priest's servant, cutting off his right ear. The servant's name was Malchus.

Judas fled.

One may agree that if Peter had been alert as the Lord had advised him—*"Could you not watch with Me one hour?"* (Matt. 26:40)—he may have not behaved this way.

Jesus took the ear of the servant and placed it back in its place, saying to Peter, *"Put your sword in its place, for all who take the sword will perish by the sword"* (Matt. 26:52).

As was His custom, the Lord was concerned about the welfare of His disciples. He asked the soldiers to let them go, since they were only after Him. The soldiers arrested Jesus, and the disciples fled: *"I will strike the Shepherd, and the sheep of the flock will be scattered"* (Matt. 26:31). The soldiers took Jesus to Annas, the high priest.

Here are some reflections on some persons involved that night:

1. Judas
   a. Our Lord gave him so many chances, such as allowing him to be one of the twelve. He had opportunities not just to see miracles but to participate in some. The Lord gave him the responsibility of carrying the money sack and buying what was needed for the poor during Passover.
   b. All these factors should have allowed Judas the ability to have more faith in Christ: *"Then Judas Iscariot, one of*

the twelve, went to the chief priests to betray Him to them"* (Mark 14:10).
   c. He betrayed Christ with a kiss. This sign of love and intimacy was altered to be a sign of animosity and betrayal. This must have been so hard on our Lord.
   d. Judas led Christ, along with the soldiers, toward Annas's house. Christ must have felt so much pain and torment when one of His "sons" not only betrayed Him with a kiss but also led Him like a "lamb" for slaughter!
2. The soldiers
   a. It is important to mention that the soldiers who made the arrest of Jesus were the high priest's soldiers and not Roman ones. Pilate was unaware of the plot up until this moment.
   b. Christ said "I am," and the soldiers fell to their knees: *"Now when He said to them, 'I am He,' they drew back and fell to the ground"* (John 18:6). Only God uses those words. They must have been familiar with the specific use of "I am," especially when Moses stood in awe listening to similar dialogue: *"He said, 'I am the God of your father—the God of Abraham, the God of Isaac, and the God of Jacob.' And Moses hid his face, for he was afraid to look upon God"* (Exod. 3:6).
3. Peter
   a. This night was Peter's worst night; he himself never imagined he would deny His Master: *"Peter said to Him, 'Even if I have to die with You, I will not deny You!'"* (Matt 26:35).
   b. Our Lord warned Peter, *"I will strike the Shepherd, and the sheep of the flock will be scattered"* (Matt. 26:31). But Peter unfortunately thought of himself better than his

brothers: *"Peter said to Him, 'Even if all are made to stumble, yet I will not be'"* (Mark 14:29).

c. Our Lord warned him for the second time: *"Assuredly, I say to you that today, even this night, before the rooster crows twice, you will deny Me three times"* (Mark 14:30). But Peter never thought he could fall that low nor deny three times in one night.

d. Our Lord warned him for the third time: *"I have prayed for you, that your faith should not fail; and when you have returned to Me, strengthen your brethren"* (Luke 22:32). It was amazing that Christ was willing to "take him back" even after he had messed up three times! That was great mercy, which Christ showed Peter and us.

e. Then Peter continued to lose focus with His master from here all the way to rock bottom. First, *"Peter followed at a distance"* (Luke 22:54). This gives us the first lesson: the strongest among us tend to fall when they follow Christ from a distance. Moreover, he mingled with the wrong crowd: *"when they had kindled a fire in the midst of the courtyard and sat down together, Peter sat among them"* (Luke 22:55). Choose the crowd you spend time with, especially when you are vulnerable.

f. Peter denied three times, but the lowest moment was when he got so scared that he started to do more than just deny: *"Then he began to curse* and *swear, 'I do not know this Man of whom you speak!'"* (Mark 14:71).

g. By the third denial and the second crowing of the rooster, Jesus looked at Peter from afar. He did that while He was in the midst of facing the Sanhedrin:

Immediately, while he was still speaking, the rooster crowed. And the Lord turned and looked at Peter. Then

THE FELLOWSHIP OF HIS SUFFERINGS

> Peter remembered the word of the Lord, how He had said to him, "Before the rooster crows, you will deny Me three times." So Peter went out and wept bitterly. (Luke 22:60–62)

This *look* was probably more like "Remember, even when you deny me, I love you, I am praying for you" rather than, "I told you so…you are not as good as you thought you were!"

h. Peter, however, was amazing; he had strong faith and hope in God's forgiveness, and that is why he repented, I wonder if he was looking forward for their private meeting at the Sea of Tiberias after His resurrection. (John 21)

DR. HANI ASHAMALLA

Meditation and a Prayer

Tell me, O you whom I love, where you feed your flock, where you make it rest at noon.

—Song of Solomon 1:7

Where do You have Your rest?
How is it I see You, Lord, and You are under arrest in Annas's house?
How can they arrest the Light?
How can they contain the Uncontainable?
With Your own authority, You permitted them to put their hands on You! This act must have shamed the angels and made them cover their faces in sadness and awe.
Lord, You are spending this night in Caiaphas's house, waiting for Your trials and Your cross.
How can I sleep in my bed?
Lord, You will spend the night with no bed, no food nor drink…how can I go eat and drink?
Lord, You are working on my vine, removing all the thorns that I placed!
Strangely, each thorn I planted, You managed to carry humbly on Your head.
Lord, have mercy on me!

The Trials of Jesus Christ

He was led as a lamb to the slaughter,
And as a sheep before its shearers is silent,
So He opened not His mouth.
He was taken from prison and from judgment,
And who will declare His generation?
For He was cut off from the land of the living;
For the transgressions of My people He was stricken.

—Isaiah 53:7–8

Our Lord was on trial in six courts. Since this was a very high-profile case, the first two trials took place at night and in secret. Both trials occurred on the eve of Friday, probably between 11:00 p.m. and 4:00 a.m.

The First Trial

The judge, Annas, is believed to have been the former high priest. He was also the father-in-law of Caiaphas, the high priest at the time.

Annas continued to have some power, even though he was not the formal high priest during Jesus's trials.

THE SECOND TRIAL

The judge here was Caiaphas, the high priest. Annas sent Jesus to Caiaphas to be tried. Caiaphas asked Jesus this question: "Are you the Son of the Most High?" Jesus answered truly, *"I am. And you will see the Son of Man sitting at the right hand of the Power, and coming with the clouds of heaven"* (Mark 14:62).

At His speech, Caiaphas theatrically tore his priestly garment to indicate his disagreement with the answer. The tearing of the priestly clothes is a despicable act before God, and according to the book of Leviticus, the Jewish priesthood fell from this point onward:

> And Moses said to Aaron, and to Eleazar and Ithamar, his sons, "Do not uncover your heads nor tear your clothes, lest you die, and wrath come upon all the people. But let your brethren, the whole house of Israel, bewail the burning which the Lord has kindled." (Lev. 10:6)

Many false witnesses were brought to testify, but none of their testimonies were valid. The only accusation that Jesus did not oppose, but rather accepted, was that *He was the Son of God.*

The high priests agreed that Jesus would be kept in Caiaphas's house to be tried (during the third trial) in the morning. According to the Jewish Talmud, it is unlawful for the Sanhedrin to conduct a trial between evening and morning. The trials were not to be conducted at night.

THE FELLOWSHIP OF HIS SUFFERINGS

The Lord spent that night (eve of Friday) in Caiaphas's house in order to be tried again in the morning. The gospel writers, including Matthew, Mark, and Luke, recorded events from that night:

- "Then they spat in His face and beat Him; and others struck Him with the palms of their hands" (Matt. 26:67).
- "Then some began to spit on Him, and to blindfold Him, and to beat Him, and to say to Him, 'Prophesy!' And the officers struck Him with the palms of their hands" (Mark 14:65).
- "Now the men who held Jesus mocked Him and beat Him. And having blindfolded Him, they struck Him on the face and asked Him, saying, 'Prophesy! Who is the one who struck you?' And many other things they blasphemously spoke against Him" (Luke 22:63–65).

In spite of what the evangelists recorded, Christ spent many hours at the hands of those soldiers, enduring tortures and humiliation that were not written or recorded. We have often wished to know more about this painful night. What was the Creator thinking as His creation mocked Him?

Meditation

"The Night That Jesus Spent in Caiaphas's House"[1]

If they do these things in the green wood, what will be done in the dry?

—Luke 23:31

Lord...
 You are the green wood.
 What did they do to You?
 What did they do to You? You have never broken a bruised reed (Matt. 12:20).
 Did they hit You with a rod?
 And You are the King holding the royal rod.
 Did they spit on You?
 And Your face makes the sun blush.
 Did they insult You and pull Your beard?
 Did they prevent You from sleeping even for one hour?
 Did they alternate in torturing You, so each team would rest a little but You could not?

---

[1] In Jerusalem, there is a church by the name of St. Peter in Gallicantu, which is thought to be the original house of Caiaphas. In the basement of that church, there are several dungeons, and this is thought to be the place where Jesus was held. It is named after St. Peter because it is thought that Peter denied the Lord in the courtyard of that house.

Lord, we now spend the night with You when You are in the tomb on the eve of Saturday. Is it Your mercy that did not want to us to spend another night with You on the eve of Friday?

Lord,
> they covered Your eyes and asked You, "Who hit You?" and You did not answer, although You are the searcher of hearts.
> You did not answer to carry the whole shame on my behalf.

Lord,
> I thank You because You let me rest, and You stay awake in Caiaphas's house until the grain of wheat falls to the ground and dies (John 12:24).

Lord,
> I will never forget where You spent that night and why.
> I know where You are, my Lord; You are there in the place that is supposed to be mine!

Lord, have mercy on me!

Routes Taken from Christ's Arrest until Golgotha (See map that follows) (Whiston 1998)

A. Toward Gethsemane on the eve of Friday (approximately 2.3 kilometers or 1.4 miles)
   1. the upper room (House of Mark)
   2. the southern gate (to be used by the Jews except for the priests)
   3. Kedron Valley
   4. Gethsemane
B. Route of the arrest of Jesus on the eve of Friday (approximately 1.82 kilometers or 1.13 miles)
   4. Gethsemane
   5. the Eastern gate (restricted to the use of the temple's soldiers)
   6. the Valley gate
   7. the Central Valley (difficult to cross because of the steep hill)
   8. Caiaphas's house (where the trials of the night and Peter's denial happened and Jesus spent the eve of Friday)
C. The route taken by Jesus Christ early morning of Friday (approximately 0.44 kilometers or 0.27 miles)
   8. Caiaphas's house (where the sentence of the nightly trials was confirmed)
   9. Pilate's palace (the fourth trial)
   10. Herod Antipas's palace (the fifth trial)
   11. Pilate's palace (the sixth trial)
D. The route toward Golgotha (approximately 1.5 kilometers or 0.9 miles)
   11. Pilate's palace

12. Gennath gate (restricted to be used only by the Roman soldiers)
13. Golgotha (outside the second walls of Jerusalem, according to Josephus)
14. The tomb of Jesus Christ

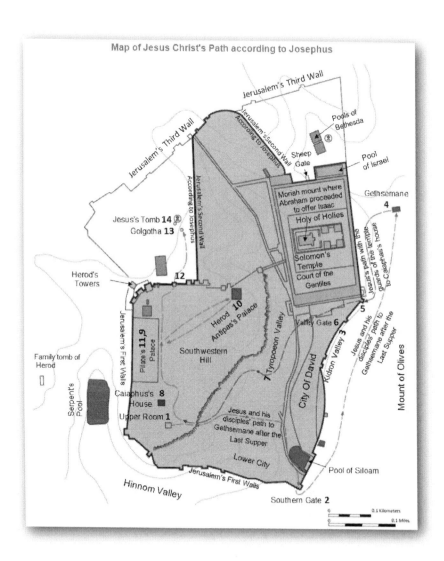

Holy Friday

He was oppressed and He was afflicted,
Yet He opened not His mouth;
He was led as a lamb to the slaughter,
And as a sheep before its shearers is silent,
So He opened not His mouth.

—Isaiah 53:7

The First Hour of Holy Friday
The Third Trial

THE THIRD TRIAL was conducted in the early hours of Friday—around six o'clock in the morning—so the high priest could confirm the decisions taken at night based on the two unlawful earlier trials. The Sanhedrin, with its seventy-one members, was generally divided between the liberal Sadducees and the more conservative Pharisees. However, that morning they were all united on one cause: Jesus must be killed. They confirmed the accusations listed the night before against Jesus, and they agreed to take Jesus (the accused) to Pilate. The latter represented the legislative and executive authority in Jerusalem and would be the one making the decision about execution.

The Fourth Trial

The high priests led Jesus to Pilate's Praetorium. They refused to enter Pilate's house lest they become defiled. Pilate's house—similar to any Gentile's house—would defile a Jew who entered. Additionally, his house would have leavened bread: *"But they themselves did not go into the Praetorium, lest they should be defiled, but that they might eat the Passover"* (John 18:29).

The irony was that they were worried about being defiled by entering a Gentile's house but were not concerned about falsifying witnesses' testimonies.

We need to search ourselves; we may be judging those high priests for their hypocrisy, and at the same time we try to be so careful about checking food ingredients in order not to break our fasting. Similarly, we may be falling into sins like gossiping or lying to take care of a certain issue, and then we go and sing, "To Thine is the power, glory, blessings…" We should work on not being hypocrites in our faith and actions.

During the fourth trial before Pilate, the high priests prepared false accusations and witnesses, but none of the testimonies were valid in Pilate's eyes.

- "I find no fault in this Man" (Luke 23:4).
- "I am innocent of the blood of this just Person. You see to it" (Matt. 27:24).
- "I find no fault in Him at all" (John 18:38).

But because of the high priest's pressure, he could not let Jesus go. He instead found a different route by sending him to Herod, the ruler of Galilee, who at this time was staying in Jerusalem because of the Passover. Pilate used the fact that Jesus was from Galilee to send him to be tried by Herod: *"When Pilate heard of Galilee, he asked if the Man were a Galilean"* (Luke 23:6). It is said that both became friends after that referral occurred (Luke 23:12). Christ was doing a conciliatory act by making enemies into friends even at the time of his crucifixion.

In the same hour, Judas regretted his actions and proceeded to hang himself.

DR. HANI ASHAMALLA

Meditation in the First Hour of Holy Friday

"Lest They Should Be Defiled"

They themselves did not go into the Praetorium, lest they should be defiled.

—John 18:28

Lord, why did the scriptures insist on including this verse in the Gospel?
   I know You do not want me to be a judge over those high priests.
   I also know that You did not mean to record this verse as a historical fact nor as a prominent event.
Lord, why did You record this statement?
   Were You pointing at me in this verse—me, coming to attend the Holy Friday service, arriving before others, carrying my books, knowing my hymns, memorizing your words… "straining out a gnat and swallowing a camel" (Matt. 23:24)?
Lord, today is a day for judgment and a day for condemnation.
   I am the one who judges, but there is no one to be judged, except me.
   I am the one who offered You to judgment, but I am still proud to be an expert on the hymns and the prayers!
   I am the one who is concerned about the purity of the body, and I suppress the Spirit
Lord, how do I appear before You as a judge when I am the accused!
   How do I appear before you singing when my lips are defiled!
Lord, have mercy on me!

The Third Hour of Holy Friday

> *From the sole of the foot even to the head, there is no soundness in it,*
> *But wounds and bruises and putrefying sores; they have not been closed or bound up, or soothed with ointment.*
>
> —Isaiah 1:6

The Fifth Trial

This is the most vicious trial out of the six. It probably occurred around 9:00 a.m. Herod Antipas—the son of Herod the Great, who had ordered the killing of the Bethlehem children—was now the ruler of Galilee (20 BC–AD 39). He wanted badly to see Jesus Christ: *"Now when Herod saw Jesus, he was exceedingly glad; for he had desired for a long time to see Him, because he had heard many things about Him, and he hoped to see some miracle done by Him"* (Luke 23:8).

When Jesus was presented before Herod and refused to show him any miracles, Herod became furious. He treated Jesus with contempt. He mocked and he tortured our Lord severely. When Herod finished, he arrayed Christ in a gorgeous scarlet robe and sent him back to Pilate.

The Coptic Church reads a very suitable prophecy at this hour from Isaiah:

> Who is this who comes from Edom,
> With dyed garments from Bozrah,
> This One who is glorious in His apparel,
> Traveling in the greatness of His strength?—
> "I who speak in righteousness, mighty to save."
> Why is Your apparel red,

> And Your garments like one who treads in the winepress?
> "I have trodden the winepress alone,
> And from the peoples no one was with Me.
> For I have trodden them in My anger,
> And trampled them in My fury;
> Their blood is sprinkled upon My garments,
> And I have stained all My robes.
> For the day of vengeance is in My heart,
> And the year of My redeemed has come.
> I looked, but there was no one to help,
> And I wondered
> That there was no one to uphold;
> Therefore My own arm brought salvation for Me;
> And My own fury, it sustained Me.
> I have trodden down the peoples in My anger,
> Made them drunk in My fury,
> And brought down their strength to the earth."
>
> —Isaiah 63:1–6

The slaves who were used to producing wine from grapes usually entered the winepress wearing clean white clothes, and after they had crushed the grapes to make the juice, they would come out from the winepress with red clothes. Jesus Christ appeared "red" at the third hour after many tortures, in addition to the thorns and flogging.

Eventually, Herod found no guilt in our Lord, so he sent Him back to Pilate.

THE SIXTH TRIAL

This trial occurred at approximately noon. Pilate tried to avoid being the final judge on Jesus, especially since he had received a message from his wife (Claudia Procula) warning him not to harm Jesus. She had seen a dream and suffered about Jesus in that dream: *"Have nothing to do with that just Man, for I have suffered many things today in a dream because of Him"* (Matt. 27:19).

Pilate's last feeble move to let Jesus free, knowing that "he found no guilt in Him," was to use a tradition available to the ruler during Passover. He would be allowed to set free one criminal chosen by the people. He placed in comparison with Jesus the worst enemy, Barabbas: *"Barabbas, who was chained with his fellow rebels; they had committed murder in the rebellion"* (Mark 15:17). He was hoping that the multitude would chose to set Jesus free, but the high priests rallied the people to shout, "Set Barabbas free and lift Jesus [on the cross]." Pilate asked them, in the manner of a ruler who had lost all authority, *"What then do you want me to do with Him whom you call the King of the Jews?"* (Mark 15:12).

Jesus was silent throughout all the trials, to the extent Pilate wished He said something: *"Are you not speaking to me? Do you not know that I have power to crucify You, and power to release You?"* (John 19:10).

Then Pilate gave Jesus to be crucified and set Barabbas free, although he had found no guilt in Jesus.

DR. HANI ASHAMALLA

Prayer after the Third Hour

I have trodden the winepress alone.

—Isaiah 63:3

Lord, why do I see you today as a slave?
Lord, you are the master, how come you accept being treated like a slave?
> A slave who has trodden the winepress and the grapes have reddened Your garment.
> You appear like a lonely slave…
> Working hard in Your own vineyard, with no one to give You a hand.

As a slave
> You passed through the *oil press*—Gethsemane—and good oil came out, healing every illness, except Yours.
> You passed through the *grape press*—the flogging, the thorns—and juice of its branches satisfied all thirst, except Yours.
> You passed through the *blood press*—the cross—and blood and water came canceling all death, except Yours.

Lord, thank You for passing through the winepress on my behalf.

Lord, have mercy on me!

Claudia Procula—Pilate's Wife

There is little mentioned about her, only that she had a dream: *"While Pilate was sitting on the judge's seat, his wife sent him this message: 'Don't have anything to do with that innocent Man, for I have suffered a great deal today in a dream because of him'"* (Matt. 27:19).

With her confession, she condemned Pilate's unfair ruling and opened the door for the Gentiles to enter God's bosom. The Ethiopian Orthodox Church celebrates Claudia's martyrdom on the twenty-seventh of October.

DR. HANI ASHAMALLA

The Sixth Hour of Holy Friday

> *But I am a worm, and no man; a reproach of men, and despised by the people. All those who see Me ridicule Me; they shoot out the lip, they shake the head, saying, "He trusted in the L*ord*, let Him rescue Him; Let Him deliver Him, since He delights in Him!"*
>
> —Psalm 22:6–8

Around 11:00 a.m., Christ started carrying His cross from Pilate's palace to Golgotha. The process of crucifixion began around noon, and darkness fell on the whole earth until 3:00 p.m.

Incense is not used in the Coptic Orthodox Church throughout the Passion Week (with the exception of Holy Thursday) until the sixth hour of Holy Friday.

The Father accepted His Son's sacrifice on the cross; He smelled it as a sweet aroma. The reconciliation with the world was completed through the sacrifice on the cross that made peace between heaven and earth. The church sings a hymn praising Christ on the cross: *"Fai etaf enf."*

This is He who presented himself on the cross; an acceptable sacrifice for the salvation of our race. His good Father inhaled His sweet aroma in the evening on Golgotha.

When the church sees her Groom suffering for her, appearing in weakness, the church sings a very strong hymn called in Coptic "Omonogennis," which says, "He is the only begotten and beloved son...He showed with weakness what is greater than bravery." This song is followed by "Agioc o Theos," or Holy God. The church, as the devoted bride, praises her Groom—that even if the whole world saw weakness in Jesus Christ, she sees Him as mighty and eternal.

The church also remembers the Virgin Mary, the mother of God, the *Theotokos*, and we sing "Tai Shouri," telling her, "You had a sword piercing your soul when you saw your Son and Lord hanging on the wood of the cross."

We read part of the epistle of Saint Paul to the Galatians: *"May I never boast except in the cross of our Lord Jesus Christ through which the world has been crucified to me, and I to the world"* (Gal. 6:14).

The Words of Christ on the Cross

What if we were to contemplate His words as if we were saying them?

"Forgive them, for they do not know what they are doing."

One said, "If Jesus was not God, he must be God when he forgave those who crucified him."

- Do I forgive as my Lord forgave?
- Do I give excuses as He did for those who crucified Him?
- Do I ask on behalf of my friends and family as He asked from His father?

"Today you will be with me in paradise."

He promised the thief on the right, "You will be with Me in paradise." He accepted his repentance and his valiant defense in the darkest times.

- Do I have hope in those I meet?
- Does my hope hold even for those who may resemble the good thief before he confessed?

"This is your son…This is your mother."

He spoke to his mother, stating that from now on John would be her son, and then He spoke to John and asked him to take care of His mother since she had no one to care for her.

- Do I make Saint Mary proud of me as her son?
- Do I make my house ready for Saint Mary to reside in?

- Am I willing to continue my struggle till the cross so I may earn the privilege of having Saint Mary living in my house?

"I AM THIRSTY."

He said, "I am thirsty," so *"they offered him wine mingled with gall, so when Jesus had received the sour wine (frequently referred to as vinegar), he did not want to drink"* (Matt. 27:48). It was customary for those being crucified to be given this drink in their last hours to dull their pain with its narcotic effect.

He did not want to drink in order to not diminish His pain, desiring to drink the cup of His sufferings to the end: *"My father, if it is possible, may this cup be taken from me. Yet, not as I will, but as you will"* (Matt. 26:39).

He wanted to offer us a complete and a perfect salvation, so He did not let anything lessen His pains.

- Do I thirst for the word of Christ and His Bible?
- Do I thirst for His body and blood?
    - It is said "Blessed are those who hunger and thirst for righteousness, for they shall be filled." Matt. 6:7), Am I being counted among those who are blessed?
    - Do I taste His word for a minute or a verse, and I refuse to be filled?

"MY LORD, MY LORD, WHY HAVE YOU FORSAKEN ME?"

These words were followed very closely or were accompanied by complete darkness on the whole earth.

- Jesus is the Light of the world.
- When He was on the cross, He was carrying the sins of the whole world, both those committed before and also after the cross.
- With Jesus as a carrier of all the sins (and not a sinner Himself), the Father hid His face from Him.
- On the cross His divinity never departed from His humanity, even for a twinkle of an eye. Upon His death, darkness filled the world that had crucified its Creator.
- Christ endured all the sufferings of the cross to offer us a perfect and complete salvation.

The words of King David, spoken almost one thousand years before the event of the cross, were accurately fulfilled: *"They pierced My hands and My feet; I can count all My bones. They look and stare at Me. They divide My garments among them and for My clothing they cast lots"* (Ps. 22:16–18).

THE FELLOWSHIP OF HIS SUFFERINGS

SIMON THE CYRENIAN

This young man, who was coming from the country...on him they laid the cross that he might bear it after Jesus (Luke 23:26).

Simon was from Cyrene (Northern Africa, possibly Libya) and had two sons (Alexander and Rufus). During the route toward Golgotha, Jesus lost so much blood and fell more than once under the weight of the cross. The Roman soldiers were afraid that He might die before He was crucified—hence the need to solicit the help of Simon to carry the cross with Jesus.

We don't know about the interaction between Simon and Jesus while they were both carrying the cross, some of the following thoughts may have happened: The fact that Simon shared in carrying the cross shows that the cross is indeed ours and Jesus never deserved it. *Simon witnessed to entire humanity that the cross is ours.*

- Every time we endure the cross of our sufferings and tribulations, we need to remember that Christ is carrying it along with us (perhaps even carrying it in front of us). This thought will help us continue on the pathway to the heavenly place.
- This is a unique time when we will be very close to Christ, carrying the cross together—hearing His words and accepting His intercession on our behalf when He is carrying our tribulations.
- Now we may fully understand the meaning of the psalmist when he said, *"I have set the* LORD *always before me; because He is at my right hand I shall not be moved"* (Ps. 16:8).
- In all my ways, as long as I do not forsake carrying my cross, I will have my Lord on my right side.

BARABBAS

Barabbas is a Hebrew name that means "son of the father." It was said about him that he was caught after committing a murder around the time of Jesus's crucifixion: *"A man called Barabbas was in prison with the insurrectionists who had committed murder in the uprising"* (Mark 15:7).

Barabbas is by far the most famous thief known to the church. His fame was due to the failed attempts of Pilate to free Jesus before the Sanhedrin after he said three times, *"I find no fault in this man"* (Luke 23:4).

Pilate used his last "card" in order to avoid the responsibility of crucifying an innocent man. He resorted to an old custom, available to him during major feasts, which gave the governor the right to release one of the prisoners.

Logically, those who would be given their freedom in Passover are the least vicious criminals. But, in order to try to free Jesus, Pilate decided to choose Barabbas, hoping that his aggression compared to Jesus's meekness would convince the crowd that Jesus should be released.

But to his dismay, *"They cried out, 'Away with him, away with him! Crucify him!' Pilate said to them, 'Shall I crucify your King?' The chief priests answered, 'We have no king but Caesar!'"* (John 19:15).

This thief found himself freed, and to his surprise, the one who took his position was the most righteous and the most holy One.

Barabbas, what did you see, and what did you observe?

- *I saw in my place—on the cross—the Lord, the Holy One.*
- *I, the real criminal, am released, and the One who had never sinned is on the cross in my place.*

- *I saw the One who is worshiped by the angels being condemned, and I, the sinful one, receiving no condemnation.*

Barabbas, in spite of his criminal history, is a living symbol for all humanity who enjoy salvation and are no longer condemned, regardless of our past actions.

DR. HANI ASHAMALLA

THE NINTH HOUR OF HOLY FRIDAY

Just as many were astonished at you, so His visage was marred more than any man, and His form more than the sons of men.

—ISAIAH 52: 14

This period lasts approximately from 1:00 p.m. until 3:00 p.m. In His last hour on the cross our Lord said, *"Father, into Your hands I commit My spirit"* (Luke 23:46).

Here, he is returning to the Father all that He has.

But from a human point of view, do I expect at the end of my life that I will say as Jesus said on the cross, "Into Your hands I commit my spirit." Lord, help me to live all my life for You so I may deserve to submit my spirit into Your hands and no other's.

It is finished.

—JOHN 19:30

I have glorified You on the earth. I have finished the work which You have given Me to do.

—JOHN 17:4

Shall I not drink the cup which My Father has given Me.

—JOHN 18:11

Christ had completed His work of salvation, and with His cross, He opened the gate of paradise for Adam and his sons to enter. He restored our sonship, which we had lost through sin.

But from a human point of view,

- Do I have a mission to complete?
- Do I have an objective to reach?
- Can I say at the end of my life that I have completed the work you have given me since "I am his workmanship created in Christ Jesus for good works" (Eph. 2:10)?

THE NINTH-HOUR HYMNS

Our Lord tasted death through His flesh on the cross in the ninth hour. Hence, many hymns are sung to depict this: "For indeed Christ, our Passover, was sacrificed for us" (1 Cor. 5:7).

We chant a Coptic song called "Fai etaf enf." He has become an acceptable sacrifice on the cross: "This is He who presented himself on the cross; an acceptable sacrifice for the salvation of our race. His good Father inhaled His sweet aroma in the evening on Golgotha."

We also chant "Agios o Theos"— "Holy God, Holy Mighty, Holy Immortal have mercy upon us."

The wise church teaches her children that even if the whole world sees in Christ a weak and dead figure, we know better. He is the Immortal God; He only tasted death by the flesh.

We also chant for Saint Mary a hymn called "Tee shouri," praising Saint Mary as the censer, remembering that "the whole world rejoices in receiving salvation, while my heart burns as I look at your crucifixion which you are enduring for the sake of all, my Son and my God" (from the ninth-hour Coptic prayers).

DR. HANI ASHAMALLA

The Eleventh Hour of Holy Friday

> *Then he brought me back to the door of the temple; and there was water, flowing from under the threshold of the temple toward the east, for the front of the temple faced east; the water was flowing from under the right side of the temple.*
>
> —Ezekiel 47:1

This occurs around 5:00 p.m. When Jesus tasted death on the cross by the flesh, three amazing things occurred concurrently:

1. **The graves were opened:** *"The graves were opened; and many bodies of the saints who had fallen were raised"* (Matt. 27:52). This is an amazing event because with Jesus's death a mass resurrection had occurred, which pointed toward the final resurrection at the end of the days.
2. **Jesus's body was pierced, and blood and water came out:** *"But one of the soldiers pierced his side with a spear, and immediately blood and water came out"* (John 19:34). Saint Augustine said, "While Adam slept in paradise, Eve came from his side, and when the second Adam slept on the cross, the church came from His side." Speaking of the two main sacramental pillars of the church, we have Baptism (water) and Eucharist (blood).
3. **When Jesus's side was pierced, the veil of the temple was torn from top to bottom:** *"Then, behold, the veil of the temple was torn in two from top to bottom; and the earth quaked, and the rocks were split"* (Matt. 27:51). *"Therefore, brethren, having boldness to enter the Holiest by the blood of Jesus, by a new and*

living way which he consecrated for us, through the veil, that is, his flesh" (Heb. 10:19–20). *"By that will we have been sanctified through the offering of the body of Jesus Christ once for all"* (Heb. 10:10). The Jews saw the Holy of the Holies for the first time in their lives when the veil of the temple was torn. For a Jew, this is the most marvelous sight. Ordinary Jews are not even allowed to imagine it, let alone see it! In addition to the utter marvel, they believed that no one could experience this and live to tell about it.

Under the cross, the centurion announced, *"This is truly the Son of God"* (Matt. 27:54) because through His death He gave life.

It is known scientifically that the blood in the vessels coagulates (becomes clotted) minutes after death; the gush of water and blood from Jesus's side after death was a sign that His humanity would not decay because of the inseparable unity with His divinity.

Meditation

The Middle Wall You Have Abolished

—Saint Gregory the Theologian

As a man, I was in God's bosom, but I fell because of my disobedience.

There was a middle wall, an enmity, between God and man. This wall was thick, and the enmity was strong.

When Jesus died on the cross and His body was pierced by the spear, the veil of the temple was torn from top to bottom, and the reconciliation between heaven and earth—God and man—was established.

It had to be torn from the top down, not from the bottom up, since man was incapable of reconciling with God. God did the whole work.

According to Saint Gregory, *"The middle wall you have removed and the old enmity you have destroyed, and you made peace between heaven and earth."*

"You have disarmed principalities and powers, making a public spectacle of them, triumphing over them in it (the cross)*"* (Col. 2:15) to save me.

Thank You, Lord, for Your pierced side.

Through this opened side, I returned to worship You as a son and not as a slave.

Thank You, Lord!

Lord, have mercy on me!

THE FELLOWSHIP OF HIS SUFFERINGS

The Twelfth Hour of Holy Friday

> *Then, behold, the veil of the temple was torn in two from top to bottom; and the earth quaked, and the rocks were split.*
>
> —MATTHEW 27:51

This occurs around 6:00 p.m. The altar is opened since the veil of the temple was torn. Now we are allowed to enter the altar, which was closed for the whole Passion Week: *"By a new and living way which he consecrated for us, through the veil, that is, his flesh."* (Heb. 10:20).

The candles are lit, and the black curtains are removed and replaced by white ones in expectation of our perfect salvation. We read a chapter from the Lamentations of Jeremiah: *"I am the man who has seen affliction by the rod of His wrath…It is good for a man to bear the yoke in his youth"* (Lam. 3:1, 27).

The Coptic Church sings a very beautiful hymn called Ⲡⲉⲕⲑⲣⲟⲛⲟⲥ "Pekethronos": "Your Throne, O God, is forever and ever" (Ps. 45:6).

The church is addressing her Lord and King, who had made a throne for Himself on the cross, from which He will be judging the whole world.

Meditation and Prayer

How can the Light be contained?
How can the tomb engulf the Author of life?
How can the Immortal taste death?
It is your sin, my soul, that made him go through all of this.
Your resurrection, my Lord, was not a miracle. You are the Resurrection and Life.
Rather, Your death was the miracle.
You had to taste death in order to crush the last enemy.

> *"He became what we are that we might become what He is."*
>
> —Saint Athanasius (ca. 296–373)

You took our humanity, including its death and shame, to give us what is yours—resurrection and life.
Through your burial, You descended, my Lord, to the bottom of our cursed earth to sanctify it.
Your tomb, my Lord, became a source of life!
Beware, my soul.
How much you hurt your kind Lord!
Do not forget what you have done with your kind Shepherd.
Do not forget that the shame that made the angels tremble was actually yours!
And the death that shook the earth and darkened nature was your death!
And the nakedness that embarrassed the angels and eclipsed the moon was your nakedness.
So, my soul, tell me: Do you realize the magnitude of the salvation?

Are you going to forget Him after this Passion Week?
Are you going to wait for another year to feel His passions?
Lord, have mercy on me!
When are you going to be sensitive toward your Groom's work for you?
When are you going to spend your life worshiping under His feet and repenting under His cross?
The wheat grain has finally fallen into the earth, suffered, and died to bring forth fruits.
My soul, are you better than your Master?
Has the time come for the servant to be better than his Master?
Humble yourself, and die with your Groom who has plowed the garden, plucked the thorns, and lifted the curse.
Die to your desires and every pride so you may bear fruit for Him.
My Lord Jesus Christ, cover me with Your love.
Lord, have mercy on me!

Christ's Timeline from Arrest to Burial

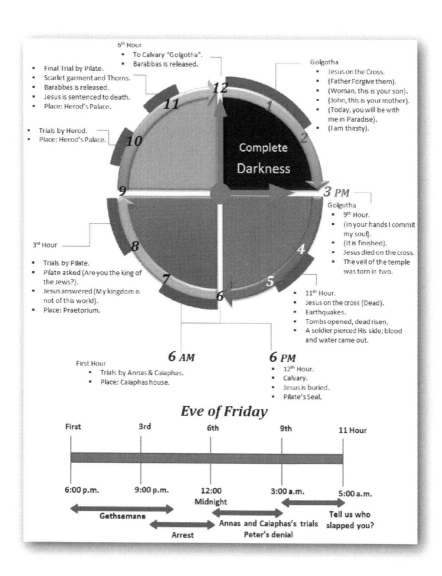

The Lord's Sufferings and Death from a Medical Perspective

Our Lord's death is a puzzle. Consider the following observations and questions.

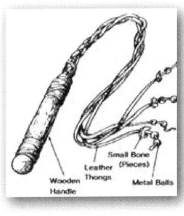

- Crucifixion does not pierce any vital organ. So what caused death?
- John declared Jesus's control over His own death: "In Your hands I submit My soul."
- How was He able to cry "with a loud voice"?
- *"Pilate marveled that He was already dead; and summoning the centurion, he asked him if He had been dead for some time"* (Mark 15:44).
- But one of the soldiers pierced His side with a spear, and immediately blood and water came out: *"But one of the soldiers pierced His side with a spear, and immediately blood and water came out"* (John 19:34).

Rigors of Ministry

- Because He traveled by foot throughout Palestine, our Lord was probably in good physical health.
- However, from 9:00 p.m. Thursday to 9:00 a.m. Friday, He was subjected to
  - physical torture;
  - sleep deprivation;
  - food and drink deprivation;
  - more than four-kilometer walk;
  - the scourge; and
  - crucifixion.

Scourging

- legal preliminary to every Roman execution
- short whip used (flagrum/flagellum)
- several braided leather thongs
- small iron balls or sharp sheep bone braided into leather
- prisoner tied to upright post
- one or two men (lictors) alternating

Medical Aspects of Scourging

- Soldiers repeatedly struck the back at full force (thirty-nine times).
- Iron balls and sheep bone would cut into the skin and subcutaneous tissue.
- Deep cuts in the skin would lead to deep tears in the skeletal muscle of the back.

- Pain and blood loss would set the stage for circulatory shock.

Biblical Accounts of Scourging

- Isaiah 52:14: "Just as there were many who were appalled at Him—His appearance was so disfigured beyond that of any man and His form marred beyond human likeness."
- Isaiah 50:6: "I offered My back to those who beat Me, My cheeks to those who pulled out My beard; I did not hide My face from mocking and spitting."

Medically, our Lord's condition was likely serious to critical.

Crucifixion Practices

- began among the Persians
- perfected by the Romans
- used as a form of torture and capital punishment
- designed to produce a slow death with maximum pain and suffering
- the most disgraceful and cruelest method of execution

The Cross (Barbet 1963)

- upright post (stipes) permanently placed in the ground
- horizontal crossbar (patibulum)
- weighed 75–125 pounds
- five to six feet long
- attached by rope and a joint

- condemned man, usually naked, carried his own patibulum from the flogging site to the crucifixion site
- Titulus (Latin word for inscription or label) showing offense of prisoner attached
- crude seat attached to stipes
- shoulder dislocated when patibulum is violently hoisted onto stipes
- prisoner given drink of myrrh and wine (served as anesthetic to make soldiers' jobs easier)
- prisoner thrown to ground and arms nailed to patibulum at the wrist (not tied)
- tapered iron spikes (five to seven inches)
- patibulum and prisoner lifted onto the stipes
- feet fixed to stipes with iron spikes
- knees at ninety-degree flexion
- Titulus then attached
- victim's belongings divided among soldiers
- victim taunted by civilian crowd
- three-hour to nine-day survival
- death hastened by crucifracture
- to confirm death, spear thrust into heart

Medical Aspects of Crucifixion

- Pre-crucifixion scourging to produce intense agony, pain, and blood loss

- Changing the garment results in reopening wounds to nail wrists when thrown to ground to the patibulum
- Each breath causes scraping against the stipes, which would continue throughout the entire crucifixion ordeal

Fixation of the Arms

- sensorimotor nerves in the hand crushed or severed by the driven nail
- excruciating bolts of fiery pain
- paralysis of a portion of the hand

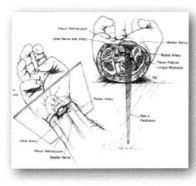

Fixation of the Feet

- between second and third toes
- severance of nerves and arteries in the foot
- pain
- additional blood loss

Respiration

- severe interference with normal respiration
- most significant cause of death on the cross
- for each breath, victim must push up on nailed feet
- pain

- nails would hit the severed nerves in hands and feet
- breathing reopens wounds on the back
- eventually, exhaustion asphyxia
- process sped up by *crucifracture*

CRUCIFRACTURE

Cruciarius is the Latin term for a victim of crucifixion: *"Because it was the Preparation Day, that the bodies should not remain on the cross on the Sabbath (for that Sabbath was a high day), the Jews asked Pilate that their legs might be broken, and that they might be taken away. Then the soldiers came and broke the legs of the first and of the other who was crucified with Him. But when they came to Jesus and saw that He was already dead, they did not break His legs"* (John 19: 31). Crucifracture results in an inability to breathe using the accessory muscles and subsequent asphyxia.

His death raises many medical and theological questions: "Many medical examiners have expressed their conclusions without recognizing that any or all of the features might embody theological description" (Edwards, Gabel, and Hosmer 1986).

CAUSES OF DEATH:

1. suffocation
2. shock
3. lung-related reasons
4. heart-related reasons

THE FELLOWSHIP OF HIS SUFFERINGS

1. Suffocation
Experiment: French surgeon Barbet (1963)

Experimentation was done on Austrian-German soldiers of World War I, who were hung alive by two hands from a post.
Findings:

- Attached by hands and legs.
- Shifts weight from hands to legs.
- Legs eventually "broken" and body slumps down.
- Intercostal muscles become exhausted.
- Lungs are filled with CO_2.
- Asphyxia.

Many disagree with that theory since our Lord died before they broke His legs, unlike the other two transgressors.

2. Shock:

    A. hypovolemic/circulatory shock (blood loss)
    B. psychological shock (grief)
    C. septic shock (infection)
    D. neurogenic shock (pain)

    A. Hypovolemic/Circulatory Shock (Blood Loss)
        1. dehydration: from 6:00 p.m. on Thursday night till 3:00 p.m. on Friday, no drinking ("I thirst!")
        2. sweating: in Gethsemane, in Caiaphas's house overnight, then while carrying the cross
        3. blood loss
        4. sweat like drops of blood (hematidrosis)

5. scourged thirty-nine times
6. hit on the head
7. nails
8. thorns
9. reopening of His back wounds by stripping His clothes
10. biblical accounts:
    i. "I am poured out like water, and all my bones are out of joint. My heart has turned to wax; it has melted away within me. My strength is dried up like a potsherd, and my tongue sticks to the roof of my mouth; you lay me in the dust of death" (Ps. 22:14–15).
    ii. "And when they had mocked Him, they took the robe off Him, put His own clothes on Him, and led Him away to be crucified" (Matt. 27:31).
    iii. "They also gave me gall for my food, and for my thirst they gave me vinegar to drink" (Ps. 69:21).
    iv. "And being in agony, He prayed more earnestly. Then His sweat became like great drops of blood falling down to the ground" (Luke 22:44).

B. Psychological Shock (Grief)
1. Jesus a very sensitive man, easily affected by emotions (e.g., Lazarus's death)
2. mental agony: Gethsemane (bloody sweat)
3. grief
4. severe vasodilatation possible, causing major drop in blood pressure and shock
5. biblical accounts:
    i. "Reproach has broken my heart, and I am full of heaviness; I looked for someone to take pity, but there was none; and for comforters, but I found none" (Ps. 69:20).

ii. "My heart has turned to wax; it has melted away within Me" (Ps. 22:14).
iii. "I was wounded in the house of my friends" (Zech. 13:6).
iv. "A Man of sorrows and acquainted with grief... Surely, He has borne our griefs, and carried our sorrows" (Isa. 53:3–4).
v. "We have turned, every one, to his own way; and the LORD has laid on Him the iniquity of us all" (Isa. 53:6).
vi. "Yet it pleased the LORD to bruise Him; He has put Him to grief" (Isa. 53:10).
vii. "And He was numbered with the transgressors, and He bore the sin of many" (Isa. 53:12).
viii. "And being in agony, He prayed more earnestly. Then His sweat became like great drops of blood falling down to the ground" (Luke 22:44).

C. Septic Shock (Tetanus)
1. Tetanus is a virulent infection classically transmitted via spores of horses' feces.
2. The nails that were used were typically taken from stables and obviously were not cleaned, which could have resulted in tetanus.
3. Tetanospasmin blocks nerve signals from the spinal cord to the muscles, causing severe muscle spasms. Spasmodic contractions can be so powerful that they tear the muscles.
4. Spasms of the respiratory and cardiac muscles could result in respiratory or cardiac death.
5. biblical accounts:
    i. "From the sole of the foot even to the head, there is no soundness in it, but wounds and bruises and

putrefying sores; they have not been closed or bound up, or soothed with ointment" (Isa. 1:6).

ii. "But He was wounded for our transgressions, He was bruised for our iniquities" (Isa. 53:5).

D. **Neurogenic Shock**
He was in severe physical pain due to the following:
1. scourging
2. hitting on the face
3. carrying the cross
4. falling under the cross
5. piercing of the nails
6. poking of the thorns
7. stripping His clothes
8. refusing anesthetics
9. biblical accounts:
    i. "For dogs have surrounded Me; the congregation of the wicked has enclosed Me. They pierced My hands and My feet; I can count all My bones. They look and stare at Me" (Ps. 21:16–17).
    ii. "He was oppressed and He was afflicted" (Isa. 53:7).
    iii. "They gave Him sour wine mingled with gall to drink. But when He had tasted it, He would not drink" (Matt. 27:34).

3. **Lung-Related Reasons (Maslen and Mitchell 2006; Mayo Clinic 1986; Zugibe 2005; Wilkinson 1989)**
    A. **Rib Fractures**
    1. Rib fractures make it very painful to take full deep breaths.
    2. This is especially worsened in the state of being suspended (as on the cross).

3. If there were multiple rib fractures, the movement of the diaphragm to take a breath will not expand the lungs because the chest wall will cave in (flail chest).
   4. This is unlikely since *"none of His bones were broken"* (Ps. 34:20).
B. **Lung Contusions**
   1. Lung contusions are like bruises on the lung tissue that render those parts of the lung ineffective in oxygen—carbon dioxide gas exchange (Barbet 1963).
   2. This prevents vital organs from having adequate oxygen levels (especially the heart and the brain), leading to tissue death in those organs.
C. **Pneumothorax**
   1. This is air in the chest that is outside of the lung, which then causes the lung to shrink in size and also leads to less effective gas exchange.
   2. Varying sizes of pneumothorax may have developed; however, it's likely they would have been small in size if they existed.
D. **Pulmonary Edema**
   1. This is fluid backing up into the lungs, which happens when the heart is not able to keep up with the stress on the body, or also when the diaphragm tries to expand the lungs unsuccessfully (negative-pressure pulmonary edema).
   2. This makes it very difficult to breathe.
   3. This may also be an explanation of the water that poured out with the blood when Our Lord's side was pierced.

4. **Heart-Related Reasons**
   A. The heart was also likely to have suffered contusions during His falls (with a 125-pound patibulum falling on his chest).

B. This leads to myocardial infarction (heart attack), loss of heart muscle, heart pump failure, and congestive heart failure—fluid backup into lungs

Heart-Failure Speculations

C. Dr. W. Stroud speculated that hemorrhage occurred through the heart wall into the pericardial sac (Jerajani et al. 2009).
D. Subsequently, the piercing resulted in blood and serum (water) gushing out.
E. These speculations were later refuted. Heart rupture does not simply occur due to mental agony.

The Mystery of Jesus's Pierced Side (Maslen and Mitchell 2006):

But one of the soldiers pierced His side with a spear, and immediately blood and water came out. And he who has seen has testified, and his testimony is true; and he knows that he is telling the truth, so that you may believe. For these things were done that the Scripture should be fulfilled, "Not one of His bones shall be broken." And again another Scripture says, "They shall look on Him whom they pierced" (John 19:34–37).

Scientific Speculations for the Blood and Water from His Side (Primrose 1949; Origen 1975):

- Scourging damaged the abdomen.
- The stomach was pierced, so blood and water came out.
- The lance hit arteries in the third intercostal space, then pierced the lungs, producing water and blood (Primrose 1949).

- Others (Litchfield 1997–1998) invalidated all theories through work with corpses dead less than twenty-four hours.
- Pericardial fluid would have to pass through the lung to exit. A fresh corpse did not exhibit that gaping tunnel.
- Pericardial sac holds only 6–7 cc of fluid.
- He was struck with a six-feet-long infantry spear
- Possibly Red Blood Cells (blood) and then plasma (water)
- It could be blood from inside the heart and fluid that was around the lungs or heart.

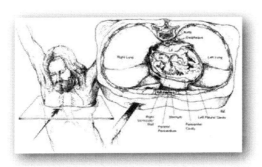

Mystery of His Death:

- Jesus's death was already established by the soldier.
- The emission of water and blood was so that "you may believe."
- He gave us life through His death.
- *"As Adam slept in paradise and Eve came out of his side, Jesus slept on the cross and the Church came from His side"* (Saint John Chrysostom).
- *"For there are three that bear witness in heaven: the Father, the Word, and the Holy Spirit; and these three are one. And there*

are three that bear witness on earth: the Spirit, the water, and the blood; and these three agree as one" (1 John 5: 7–8).

"In Your hands, I submit My soul."

- Jesus had full control over His own death.
- Jesus answered Pilate, *"You could have no power at all against Me unless it had been given you from above"* (John 19:11).
- *"And bowing His head, He gave up His spirit"* (John 19:30). He bowed His head before death—in contrast to normal death where the reverse occurs.

BIBLIOGRAPHY

1- Mark Allan Powell, 2009. " A Historical, Literary, and Theological Survey, Baker Academic, a division of Baker Publishing Group.

2- Litchfield, W. Reid. 1997–1998. "The Search for the Physical Cause of Jesus Christ's Death." *BYU Studies* 37 (4).

3- Whiston, William, trans. 1998. *The Complete Works of Josephus*, 8th ed. Nashville, TN: Thomas Nelson.

4- Saint Athanasius (ca. 296–373) on Christ's incarnation.

5- Barbet, Pierre. 1963. *The Passion of Our Lord Jesus Christ as Described by a Surgeon.* Garden City, NY: Image Books.

6- Edwards, William D., Wesley J. Gabel, and Floyd E. Hosmer. 1986. "On the Physical Death of Jesus Christ." *JAMA* 255 (11): 1455–63.

7-Jerajani, H. D., Bhagyashri Jaju, M. M. Phiske, and Nitin Lade. 2009. "Hematohidrosis—A Rare Clinical Phenomenon." *Indian Journal of Dermatology* 54 (3): 290–92.

8- Primrose, W. B. 1949. "A Surgeon Looks at the Crucifixion." *Hibbart Journal* 47 (4): 382–88.

9- Stroud, William. 1986. *On the Physical Death of Jesus Christ and Its Relation to the Principles and Practice of Christianity.* London: Hamilton and Adams.

10- Maslen, Matthew, and Piers D. Mitchell. 2006. "Medical Theories on the Cause of Death in Crucifixion." *Journal of the Royal Society of Medicine* 99:185–88.

11- Origen, A. D. 1975. "The Incident of the Blood and Water in John 19:34." *Scottish Journal of Theology* 28:159–60.

12-Edwards, W.D., Gabel, W.J., Hosmer, F.E. (1986). " on the physical death of Jesus Christ", Journal of the American Medical Association 225 1455-63.

13-Zugibe, F. T. 2005. *The Crucifixion of Jesus: A Forensic Enquiry.* New York: M. Evans.

14-Wilkinson, David. 1989. "A Ball the Crucifixion and Death of a Man called Jesus." *Journal of the Mississippi State Medical Association* 30:80–82.

Symbolic Theatrical Plays

O Christ's Wounds…Wound Me with His Love

What Have You Seen, and What Have You Observed?

His Cross or Mine?

DR. HANI ASHAMALLA

"O Christ's Wounds…Wound Me with His Love"

What if the wounds of Christ were allowed to speak?

VOICE: Many, many years ago, there was a very famous artist. He was one of the best. One day, he wanted to paint a scene of the cross. He saw hundreds of pictures before he made his first brushstroke. When he started painting, he began with the wounds of Christ. He began painting the whip, but he really wanted to know how it felt—not Christ's back but the mind of the whip. Then he said, "Let me start with an easier wound—the nails." He began painting, but he stopped. He wanted to know again how it felt. Not for Christ but for the steel. I know it sounds strange, but as an artist he could not proceed and instead kept tearing one paper after the other until he got tired and slept next to all his incomplete work.

ARTIST: I want to draw the best picture. If only I can know how they felt…not only the nails and whip but all the rest!

(NAILS and WHIP enter.)

NAILS: This artist has finally asked the question we had been hoping someone would think to ask!

WHIP: How have we felt for the past two thousand years? Do you think we will be able to really say what happened?

NAILS: I know it is difficult, but we have to try! People must know that we have feelings too!

WHIP: I was the first of all of you to lay a lash on Him or touch His body! I was resting on a table until a Roman soldier with a very strong hand came and almost choked me!

NAILS: And then what happened?

WHIP: As you can see, he made me into three leather hands; each one of these touched His back thirty-nine times. At times one of my hands would be stuck to His body, but the soldier would snatch me, and I would cut into His flesh, and his blood would stain my hands

NAILS: Why? Because you loved Him?

WHIP: I wish I had loved Him more. I would cut my hands before they touched Him!

NAILS: So why did you tear into His back?

WHIP: He created me as a nice rope made out of leather. I was supposed to help a lady pack furniture or an old man carry his stuff on a donkey!

NAILS: So why did you become like that—an instrument of pain?

WHIP: Man.

NAILS: Man?

WHIP: I am a creation of God's hands, but man took me and turned me into a tool to hurt and torture…and the first person I hurt and tortured was my own Creator.

NAILS: But how did it feel—I mean, hurting Him?

WHIP: You are really opening all my wounds again! Each time one of my hands, which are called flagrum, touched Him, He would grimace or scream, and a shock would travel through my threads. I would try to curl on myself to hurt my hands or the soldier's hand so that I wouldn't hurt Him again, but

	the soldier would straighten me and scourge Him again and again! Enough! Enough, I can't speak any more—but you keep asking me questions as if you are innocent!
NAILS:	I…I mean, we, because we are three nails…initially we were just a big piece of metal buried in the belly of the earth.
WHIP:	So He also created you?
NAILS:	Not only that, but He made me from a beautiful hard material—hard to break or twist.
WHIP:	But you always looked like this?
NAILS:	I wish I would have stayed all my life in the depths of the earth and never come out and looked like this.
WHIP:	So who made you like this?
NAILS:	Man.
WHIP:	Again, man?
NAILS:	Man took me and placed me in the fire until I was about to melt. Then he started hitting and shaping a large piece to make heads for the three of us and pointy legs like this.
WHIP:	Wow, you actually went through a lot—even more than I went through! They only made some knots in my hands and braided pieces of bone in the middle of my leather, but I wish I had gone through fire and burned and never touched my Creator's back.
NAILS:	Do you call the fire torture? I wish I had melted and been thrown away! The real torture was when I had to go through the flesh of His hands and feet!
WHIP:	What do you mean by real torture?
NAILS:	When I saw what they wanted to do with me, I kept twisting in their hands and hurting my own body

	because the hammer would come on my side rather than my big head.
WHIP:	And why would you do that?
NAILS:	I would have done anything to not hurt the Hands that had created me. I wanted to prevent my pointy legs from piercing the body of my Creator.
WHIP:	But you did hurt Him—just like me!
NAILS:	We tried, but then each one of us was held so tight by a soldier, while another hammered us. They hit us without mercy each time.
WHIP:	Without mercy—on you?
NAILS:	No, we are used to that hard treatment. But Him... they showed no mercy on his hands and feet. We could not twist or turn away. There was nothing to do except go through the skin and flesh of our Creator.
WHIP:	I hurt His back, and you went through His hands!
NAILS:	I have never seen hands like these—they did so much good! They had healed. They had created. And they were kind and wiped tears. But now we were hurting them and making them bleed, nailing them to the cross and fixing them without kindness.
WHIP:	One of you also went through both His feet, correct?
NAILS:	Yes, I did. When I was on earth, many feet stepped on me. Some I hurt, and they bled while cursing me, but for the first time in my life, I hurt feet that never walked to any bad place, feet that went to places to help all. He never cursed me while I was hurting Him!
WHIP:	Calm down, my friend. You did not have a choice!

NAILS: I wish we were not hard steel. We wish we had melted or been broken so we wouldn't have hurt our Creator.

WHIP: But I am sure He allowed all these sufferings. If He had wanted, He would have easily made you melt and me break!

(THORNS enter the scene.)

THORNS: Truly, truly, He accepted all these wounds!

NAILS: Welcome, Mr. Thorn. You were on the top! The best place, a place of honor! You had the highest rank!

THORNS: My rank was always under the feet and without honor. I was supposed to have never been created!

WHIP: Sorry, I don't understand.

THORNS: Before Adam sinned, there were none of us—only good plants. My family had never existed before.

NAILS: So how did you come to be on earth?

THORNS: When Adam sinned, God cursed the earth and said it was going to produce thorns. Since that time, the earth has produced thorns, and my family is one of the oldest! We are always reminding humans with our painful pricks that sin brings pain!

NAILS: Wow, so you are as old as I am! I have also been in the depths of the earth for thousands of years.

THORNS: Don't think I am proud of myself! You were saying I was in the place of honor, but believe me when I tell you that I allowed at least thirty thorns of my body to be broken so that I didn't pierce the head of my Creator.

WHIP:	I think I remember that same soldier who came to pick me up. Was he trying to make a crown out of you?
THORNS:	I looked at his eyes. I understood they wanted to mock my Creator and make Him appear as a king by putting me on His head, so I had to do something!
NAILS:	What did you do?
THORNS:	I made one of my longest thorns prick him. He cursed me…(laughs). I am used to that anyway. I told you, I am born because of the cursed earth.
WHIP:	But he did not leave you alone, did he?
THORNS:	No. He got his sword and started cutting me into pieces!
WHIP:	But did you let him?
THORNS:	The only thing I was able to do was to keep breaking my thorns so that he would leave me alone.
Whip:	But I saw you from the left-nail side. When I looked up, you were big and scary!
THORNS:	The largest crown of thorns ever made. Again, don't think that I am proud of that.
WHIP:	But still, how did you feel when you touched His head?
THORNS:	Electric shock! The moment each thorn touched His head, I receive a huge shock, which passed through all my branches. But when His blood stained me and fell on the earth, I felt it immediately.
NAILS:	What do you mean by "felt it"? Felt what?
THORNS:	The curse, my friends, the curse. When He bore me on His head, He carried the curse; actually, He became a curse like me, sadly.
WHIP:	So what happened to the curse now?

THORNS:	When His blood touched me and stained the earth, the curse was lifted. This is my actual honor.
NAILS:	Of course, you are honored like the best of all the wounds. There isn't a crucifixion picture without a crown of thorns.
THORNS:	God is amazing. He did not want me to always be ashamed. He replaced my curse with a blessing and honor.
WHIP:	But what did you see while you were up there—I mean, on his head?
THORNS:	Amazing—what I heard was amazing! I thought at first that He was looking at me and was going to blame me for the wounds I had caused on His forehead, but then I understood that He was looking toward His Father through my thick thorns. Then He spoke, saying, "Father, forgive them!"
NAILS:	Right, I heard him. I thought He was speaking about us—I mean us, the three nails—asking God to forgive us for the wounds we inflicted on his body.
THORNS:	Maybe. Maybe He was asking God for all of us who caused His wounds that we be forgiven. But I think He was asking for forgiveness for all the people who had made each one of us a tool for His torture, although we are His creation and the design of His hands also.

(CROSS enters the scene.)

CROSS:	His creation and the design of His hands. Yes! His creation and the design of His hands.
THORNS:	Great, here comes the one who carried all of us.

CROSS:	I carried all of you? That day, I carried the lightest weight any tree would ever carry.
WHIP:	Tree? Were you—excuse me, I don't mean this as an insult—but were you a tree?
CROSS:	Of course. I was a tree in the forest of Jerusalem. The youngest of us was a couple of hundred years old. Then one day a man came.
THORNS:	Man?
NAILS:	Man?
WHIP:	Man?
CROSS:	A man came and cut me by my roots. I heard that my other brother trees were made into small logs to warm a house or make tables or chairs. I wish I had been used for warming a house or made into the worst chair rather than becoming a cross to torture the One who had designed me and created me.
THORNS:	Tell us what happened.
CROSS:	They cut me into two big logs: one long one of about eight feet and a shorter one of five feet, but this one weighed about a hundred pounds. I also heard they made two other crosses from my two tree brothers.
WHIP:	So there were many crosses that day?
CROSS:	There were three crosses.
WHIP:	And which one of the three were you?
CROSS:	I wish I had been bad wood so they would have rejected me, but I was the best out of my brothers. They chose me to carry my Creator, and they placed the other two crosses on my sides.
THORNS:	Correct, I saw the other two crosses; they carried the thieves, right?

CROSS: But what happened to me was different from any of you! My Creator carried me for hours all the way to Golgotha. You cannot imagine my feelings when He fell under me. Actually, I am afraid to say when I... when I fell on Him. (Cries)

WHIP: Please try to tell us, we need to know!

CROSS: Our Lord was getting very weak; I am sorry to say that it was because of you, Mr. Thorns, and especially you, Mr. Whip.

WHIP: True. Just because of me, He may have lost two liters of blood!

THORNS: And because of me He had so much pain.

CROSS: So when He started carrying me, He was already very weak! I listened to his breathing. He was panting; His hands were shaking around my waist. Then one time He tripped and fell on the ground. I tried to push myself so that I didn't fall on Him, but a Roman soldier pushed me, forcing me to fall on Him. I couldn't believe it. How could I have done that? I, who had been beautifully made by His hands, dared to fall on Him?

CROSS: I don't want to hurt your feelings more, but humans say on every Holy Friday that He was crushed. Could they be speaking about you when you fell on him?

CROSS: I don't know if humans realize that they used each of us, especially me, to wound Him for them to be saved. They should know that I crushed Him for their sins. Again, I wish I had just been burned and turned to ashes rather than have crushed Him under my weight.

WHIP: What happened when you arrived at Golgotha?

THE FELLOWSHIP OF HIS SUFFERINGS

CROSS: Why do you want to remind me? Anyway, when we arrived there, they put me down and laid our Creator on me! To tell you the truth, before they put any of you nails in Him, this was the best five minutes in the life of any tree! My grandparents would dream that the hand of the Creator would touch them, and I…I had Him lying on me! For a minute, I thought He missed me; it was as if He wanted to hug me, as if He had waited for me for years.

WHIP: Don't you think you're giving yourself more credit than you deserve?

CROSS: Maybe, but believe me, I felt His breathing and His heartbeat changing as soon as He saw me, as if I were an old friend or a joy set before Him.

THORNS: Then what happened?

NAILS: You know what happened afterward. They took us and pierced His hands until we were fixed in you, Mr. Cross. I am sorry, Mr. Cross, that we hurt you. I mean, three big nails going through you must have been very painful!

CROSS: I actually did not feel you or any pain at all. Frankly, I think when you went through His flesh first and His blood stained me, I was numb and unaware of any pain but His. You guys may not know this, but as a tree, when a drop of morning dew would fall on me, I used to feel refreshed. So imagine the effect His blood had on me! I can't describe my feelings when His blood stained me.

THORNS: But He had lost so much blood by then to the extent that He said, "I am thirsty."

(SPONGE enters the scene.)

SPONGE: He was thirsty; He thirsted for water but also thirsted for every soul to be saved.

CROSS: Are you the sponge of wine?

SPONGE: I wish I were good wine; I would have been more merciful on His thirst. But I was vinegar mixed with bitterness.

THORNS: Frankly, I wanted to ask you why you came to the cross at that hour anyway.

SPONGE: It was an old custom at any crucifixion to give victims this type of drink before they died to numb their pain so they wouldn't scream or curse during their last hours.

CROSS: But He never cursed. On the contrary, He forgave those who had crucified Him.

THORNS: And when He cried out, He only did so to submit His soul into His Father's hands.

WHIP: But His pains were intense. Maybe you should have helped Him.

SPONGE: But when He tasted me, He refused to drink.

THORNS: Yes, I saw you when they raised you on a hyssop to reach His lips. By mistake they hit me. Frankly, your touch stings a lot. But why did He not want to drink?

SPONGE: He refused to drink because He did not want anything to reduce His pain.

THORNS: But why?

CROSS: He wanted to drink the cup of His pain to the last drop to save all His people.

SPONGE: That is why He did not want to drink from you…so His pain would be perfect and complete.

(SPEAR enters the scene.)

THE FELLOWSHIP OF HIS SUFFERINGS

SPEAR: You all were part of His sufferings when He was alive, but I am very different.
CROSS: Ah, I know you. I saw you. You are the spear, right?
SPEAR: Yes, I am the spear. Longinus, the Roman captain, used me to prove that he had died.
THORNS: I was afraid they were going to have to break his legs.
SPEAR: No way. The prophecy had to be fulfilled that said, "None of His bones will be broken!"
CROSS: No way. He said none of His bones will be broken?
SPEAR: I was standing on the side, leaning and watching all His sufferings. I was like you, nails; I wished also to have melted or twisted before being used to wound my Creator. But then I saw Longinus, who was a good soldier. He had to prove to Pilate that He had died, so he came to grab me!
THORNS: And then what happened?
SPEAR: He thrust me from below into His right side, going deep into his heart, and all of a sudden, there was a gush of water and blood, which stained me and Longinus to the extent that Longinus threw me down and screamed, saying, "This is truly the Son of God."
WHIP: But why did He say that?
SPEAR: As a Roman soldier who was used to seeing dead people, he was amazed when the dead Lord bled like this. He screamed when he heard Him forgiving His crucifiers and when he saw blood and water coming from His side after His death.

(WHIP, NAILS, THORNS, CROSS, SPONGE, and SPEAR all gather. The ARTIST quickly starts to work on putting them together in the painting.)

ARTIST: Every wound inflicted on Christ is man-made, and every creation God made to please man, man used them to wound His Creator. Oh, man, are you still wounding your Creator? Are you still using what *He* granted you to live well, or do you use what was granted to you to hurt and wound the One who created you? If those things that hurt Christ felt His pains, even though they were not living elements, how much more did you feel? How could you not appreciate what He has done for you and continues to do? Oh, wounds of Christ, wound me with the love of the One who died for me!

What Have You Seen, and What Have You Observed?

A symbolic operetta about Claudia Procula

(CHRIST is wearing the thorns and a scarlet robe. He has been flogged, and His back is toward us. He is facing PILATE. CLAUDIA is standing to the side.)

PILATE: Speak! Don't You know that I have the authority to release You and the authority to crucify You!

CHRIST: You have no authority over Me unless you are given this from above.

PILATE: Are you a king?

CHRIST: Is that what you are saying yourself or because of what others have told you about me?

PILATE: If you were a king, then where is Your kingdom?

CHRIST: My kingdom is not of this world; if it were...

(PILATE receives a letter from CLAUDIA.)

PILATE: Take Him away!

(CHRIST is taken away. He looks at CLAUDIA on His way out.)

PILATE: Claudia, why did you come here? How can your sensitive heart see this horrible scene?

CLAUDIA: It won't be worse than what I saw last night.

PILATE *(holding the message)*: Claudia, what do you mean by this message: "Watch out for this Righteous Man;

	I have suffered in a dream because of Him this night"?
CLAUDIA:	Pilate, I could not sleep the whole night because of Jesus, the One you are about to judge!
PILATE:	How come?
CLAUDIA:	I saw Him in a dream.
PILATE:	Dream? What did you see?
CLAUDIA:	I saw Him as a king! Actually, as a great king, greater than you—no, greater than Caesar and greater than the Pharaohs of Egypt!

(PILATE goes outside.)

CLAUDIA:	Greater than any king…but a sad king. In the dream, I asked Him, "Why, oh great King, are you are very sad?" Then He answered me, saying that He was sad for His people because He loved them, but they hated Him. Instead of worshiping their great King, they judged Him as if He were their servant and they were the masters.

(CLAUDIA is in front of the cross. LONGINUS enters.)

LONGINUS:	Lady Claudia, did you ask to see me?
CLAUDIA:	Longinus, thank you for coming so quickly.
LONGINUS:	Your requests are my orders, my lady.
CLAUDIA:	Can you please forget that I am Pilate's wife and that you are a Roman soldier?
LONGINUS:	My La…I mean, Claudia, what do you wish to know?
CLAUDIA:	You were under His cross—no, no, you were in charge of his crucifixion. So, tell me. What did you see, and what did you observe?

THE FELLOWSHIP OF HIS SUFFERINGS

LONGINUS: I saw...I saw the amazing, the Righteous, crucified between the thieves.

CLAUDIA: How come? What did you see, and what did you hear?

LONGINUS: I heard Him when He forgave His crucifiers, of whom I am the second after Pontius Pilate! I saw Him when I pierced His side with my own hands.

CLAUDIA: What? You pierced Him?

LONGINUS: They had to die before the Sabbath. So we broke the legs of the other two! But when I came to do the same to Him, I found Him already dead. I had to be sure, although I was already sure. Those were the orders.

CLAUDIA: Then what happened?

LONGINUS: I pierced His side, and I was soaked with blood. I mean, a lot of water and blood came out of His side. He was thirsty, but he poured out water to wash all His creation! His blood cleansed me from all my sins! He was dead and alive at the same time...so...

CLAUDIA: So, what? Please tell me everything.

LONGINUS: So, I screamed, saying, "This is truly the Son of God." There was no question about it!

CLAUDIA: I knew He was righteous. I saw Him redeeming many. But what are you saying? "He is the Son of God"? He is the dead who is giving life to all. I need to know more about Him. Longinus, please help me!

LONGINUS: You warned Pilate. You deserve to know more. You will see and hear from those around Him.

(PETER enters, holding a fishing net.)

LONGINUS: Come in, Peter. This is Claudia, Pilate's wife!

(PETER tries to leave.)

CLAUDIA	*(grabs PETER)*: Please wait. I know that my being the wife of Pilate, the one who crucified the righteous, is not helping here!
PETER:	Righteous…it is strange, isn't it, that Queen Claudia speaks about my Lord Jesus Christ as righteous. How come?
CLAUDIA:	I am willing to tell you if you promise to tell me what you observed and what you saw.
PETER:	I saw Him transfigured on the Mount of Tabor in His glory and the glory of His Father. I saw Moses and Elijah; the most important figures in our law and prophets bowing down to Him. What about you, my lady? What did you see and observe?
CLAUDIA:	I saw Him! I saw Him in a dream and also in glory better than the sun itself. Glorified but very sad…sad because He had been rejected. In my dream, I suffered when I saw Him glorified but not appreciated. Glorified but insulted.
PETER:	Moses and Elijah were speaking with him about the hour of his departure from the world. He was speaking with Moses about the true exodus, not just the exodus from Egypt…they were speaking about His pain as a silent Lamb about to be slaughtered to let us all free.

(DIMAS, the thief on the right, enters with LONGINUS.)

LONGINUS:	You? How did you come? Didn't you die on the cross?
PETER:	Welcome, Dimas.

THE FELLOWSHIP OF HIS SUFFERINGS

CLAUDIA: Dimas! Were you the thief who was crucified with Jesus?

DIMAS: Yes, I am, and you are right, Master Longinus. I did die before your eyes. But God sent me to answer a question. Then I will go back to paradise.

CLAUDIA: What did you see, and what did you observe?

LONGINUS: I could not believe my ears when I heard you saying...

DIMAS *(interrupts)*: "Remember me, oh Lord, when You come into your kingdom."

CLAUDIA: How come? If you had seen Him like Peter in His glory at Mount Tabor, it would have been OK, but you have seen Him in weakness. What did you see, and what did you observe?

DIMAS: I will tell you on one condition. You must tell me what you saw in your dream.

LONGINUS: The day has come when a thief gives conditions to his lady!

PETER: You can say that again; the church today places the thief as her teacher on how to repent!

CLAUDIA: True. The whole church today is screaming after you, "Remember me, oh Lord, when You come into Your kingdom."

DIMAS: I saw forgiveness for those who did not deserve any forgiveness. I saw Him saying, "Father, forgive them," while we were all mocking Him, and I was the first. I saw nature complaining. I saw...no, I could not see because of full darkness. No sun, no moon, and no stars...in the middle of the day! That can only happen if the Creator of nature is suffering. I saw and heard Him telling His Father that His job had been completed.

CLAUDIA: And I saw Him as the Holy One. Amazing! The One who is worshiped by the angels was rejected and humiliated by humans. I saw Him as a Judge, a very fair Judge! Kings stand trembling before Him, and humans are judging Him, saying He was condemned.

LONGINUS: At the cross, they told Him to free Himself and come down if He was indeed the Son of God, but He endured everything, including the shame of the cross.

(MARY enters. PETER is guiding her.)

LONGINUS: You are His mother…Mary, right? I saw you under His cross. This is Claudia, Pilate's wife.

CLAUDIA: Please do not hate me.

MARY: My daughter, I do not know how to hate.

CLAUDIA: But my husband was the one who condemned your Son to death.

MARY: My daughter, your husband had no authority over Him unless it was given from above. You see, my Son was always speaking about a certain hour, even as a child, and during the wedding of Cana, He told me, "My hour has not come yet."

CLAUDIA: So He knew?

MARY: He was seeing the cross before Him all His life. Sometimes I thought He was looking forward to it, as an old friend longs for a hug.

CLAUDIA: That's what I saw in my dream. I saw Him joyful. Joyful in spite of His pain. He was pleased with the cross in the midst of His maximum pain. He was joyful, as if it were completed.

MARY: His last words on the cross were "It is done." His mission, our salvation, was completed with His last breath on this earth.

CLAUDIA: But why? Why did He make me have this dream? Why me? I could not help Him.

MARY: My daughter, He was not asking for your help or anyone's help. He was going through the winepress alone, and no one was with Him.

CLAUDIA: So why…why?

MARY: So that you will witness for Him in all the gospels. The whole world will know that the honorable lady of the Roman Empire is saying that He is righteous, even if the Jews and Romans have crucified Him.

PETER: Now, not only are we disciples witnesses but you, my lady, the lady of the Roman palace, are a witness, too.

LONGINUS: And the whole world will know that Claudia, Pilate's wife, is a saint and was martyred in Jesus's name.

PETER: And the Ethiopian and Eastern Orthodox churches will celebrate her martyrdom on the twenty-fifth of October every year as a witness who died for Christ.

"His Cross or Mine?"

(The curtain opens on a large wooden cross. There is a robe hung on it. A thorny crown and three nails have been fixed on the cross. BARABBAS walks in toward the congregation. After a greeting, he begins.)

BARABBAS: I am Barabbas. I killed and stole. I was arrested, and on the day of my execution, I was set free on the same day of my trial. They gave a choice to the people between me and another criminal. His name was Jesus. I knew of all the chief thieves, but Jesus…never heard of Him. Why did they choose Him over me? *(He turns to talk to the cross).* He must be a worse criminal than me!

VOICE: Barabbas, Barabbas…you want to know why you were set free…I will show you why they chose Me over you…I will show you whom you need to follow.

(SHEPHERDS ONE, TWO, THREE, and FOUR walk in from the middle corridor.)

SHEPHERD ONE: We are the shepherds of Bethlehem
SHEPHERD TWO: Thirty-three years ago, we were on our watch in the night.
SHEPHERD THREE: We saw Him—a little baby but full of glory!
SHEPHERD FOUR: It was a cold night; we all went to the manger.
SHEPHERD ONE: Angels and ranks of Heaven praised Him.
SHEPHERD TWO: They said, "Glory to God in the highest. Goodwill toward men."

SHEPHERD THREE: He came to give peace to people who lack peace—like you, Barabbas!

(MARY Magdalene enters with big earrings.)

BARABBAS: My lady, why was He crucified instead of me?
MARY: Barabbas!
BARABBAS: Mary? From Magdala, correct?
MARY: Yes, I am Mary the Magdalene. Remember when we met many years back in Magdala?
BARABBAS: You look very different…no drinks, less jewelry, no makeup.
MARY: The Mary you knew is dead. Jesus changed me!
BARABBAS: Why did He die instead of me?
MARY: He always loved the sinners. He opened the eyes of the blind. He raised the dead. He forgave me, and I am the most sinful.
BARABBAS: Where were you at the time of the trial?
MARY: I saw the priests inflaming the crowd to say, "Crucify Him. Crucify Him." I heard Pilate saying, "Which one do you want free—Jesus or Barabbas?" I am sorry, but I never thought any rational mind would prefer you over Christ.
BARABBAS: Did you have to be that frank? But this is what is making me go crazy. You know, if it were Dimas, I would have said it could have been OK, but Jesus… He does not look like one of us!
MARY: Under His cross, I touched the nail in His feet, and His blood cleaned me. He came for you and me!
BARABBAS: Me? How can anyone come for a person like me? Why? I must understand.

MARY: Stay near the cross, and you will understand!

(MARY takes off her earrings and puts them under the cross, then moves next to the chorus.)

BARABBAS: Why did they chose Him over me? Could He be a greater criminal than me?

(PETER enters, carrying a fishing net.)

BARABBAS: Peter, I was waiting for you. You are like me. I mean, you are tough like me.

PETER: I denied Him. I denied Him. I denied Him when He needed me the most. I cursed and said I didn't know the man. I denied Him in front of a servant.

BARABBAS: But why did you do that? Did He upset you in anything?

PETER: He upset me. He made me walk on water. When I was about to drown, he picked me up. One time, he made me fish, and when I opened that fish, I found a coin. I paid the tax for both of us. He gave me a name among the fishermen when He made me catch so many fish.

BARABBAS: So your story ended with your denial?

PETER: Strangely, He warned me that I would deny Him, but I did not listen. He told me that before the rooster crowed I would deny Him, and I did not understand. He told me to take care of my brothers when I returned, and I did not heed.

BARABBAS: Peter, what happened after the resurrection? Was He ready to see your face a second time?

PETER: When I saw Him after the resurrection, He asked me, "Do you love Me?"

BARABBAS: He asked you if you love Him? Wasn't it supposed to be you asking if He still loves you?

PETER: He did not want to embarrass me, so He asked me first and accepted me and forgave me. He told me to tend to His sheep.

BARABBAS: Are you trying to tell me that He was ready to accept you after all you had done? Can He accept you after you left Him in the time of His need? So when they cried to free Barabbas, He was as aware of who I was as He was aware of your denial? So why was He silent? If He had opened His mouth, I would have been in His place—crucified!

PETER: He was silent to defend you and me. Stay next to the cross, and you will understand.

(PETER leaves his net under the cross and moves next to the chorus.)

BARABBAS: Why did they chose Him over me? Could He be more righteous than all?

(NICODEMUS enters in Jewish rabbinical clothes.)

NICODEMUS: He told me about baptism, but I didn't understand. I am Nicodemus, one of the Jewish scholars, and I still didn't understand.

BARABBAS: But how come you never said anything when He was arrested?

NICODEMUS: Don't make it worse for me. I was scared for my job with the Sanhedrin. I followed from afar, and I was scared to be seen with Him.

BARABBAS: Don't be harsh on yourself; you were the main person during the burial.

NICODEMUS: I was joined by Joseph—Joseph of Arimathea—when He died on the cross. I asked Pilate for His body, and he granted my wish.

BARABBAS: That is very brave of you to go to Pilate. What did you see at His burial?

NICODEMUS: We saw and heard marvels. We heard angels praising, saying, "Holy God, Holy Mighty, and Holy Immortal."

BARABBAS: Holy Immortal...while you were burying Him? How could that be?

NICODEMUS: He may be dead in the eyes of everyone, but in the eyes of His church, He is immortal. On the cross, Christ showed with His weakness, what is greater than bravery! Soldiers were still scared of Him even when He was nailed.

BARABBAS: But if He died instead of me on the cross, He cannot be holy, right? Maybe He deserved the cross?

NICODEMUS: He gave you your freedom, but don't ever say He deserved the cross! You and I deserve the cross, but He does not!

(DIMAS enters through the center corridor.)

BARABBAS: Dimas! Finally I've found someone who can understand me. You are also a criminal like me. Tell me,

DIMAS: Dimas. What did you see while you were next to Him? I was supposed to be next to you, not Him! How come? Explain to me. Why, Dimas? Why did He take my place? Why did they choose Him over me?

DIMAS: He was crucified next to me. I was also mocking Him. But I heard and saw wonders! When I saw the sun and the moon shut their lights, I was so scared on the cross and in darkness. It was so dark and cold on top of the cross. The only thing that made me calm was listening to his breathing next to me.

BARABBAS: I hope you are not jealous because I was freed and you were not.

DIMAS: After what I saw and heard, believe me, I am the winner here. Even if I was given my freedom, I would have chosen these three hours next Him. All my life I was scared of dying on the cross until I found Him next to me. The cross became a bed. But when I heard Him saying "Father, forgive them because they don't know what they are doing," I thought, *How can anyone forgive His enemies, the people who crucified us?* I wanted to scream "Leave Him alone! He is Holy!" but my voice was weak. But He heard me! I said, "Remember me when You come into Your kingdom."

BARABBAS: So you do not think He deserves the cross? OK, so why did He take my place?

DIMAS: You are getting closer…stay next to the cross, and you will understand!

(CHILD ONE, TWO, THREE, and FOUR walk in through the side corridor, waving their palms or tree branches.)

BARABBAS: Girls, don't you remember me? I am Barabbas. All kids are scared of my name and my crimes. Jesus took my place on the cross. They gave Him the title of King of the Jews. Can He be more righteous than all?

CHILD ONE: When He entered Jerusalem, we were there!

CHILD TWO: No one taught us what to sing.

CHILD THREE: But we gathered in thousands, all rejoicing for the King of Israel.

CHILD FOUR: He sat on a donkey, and we all followed.

CHILD ONE: We said, "Hosanna in the highest."

CHILD TWO: We loved Him. He was different from all the other rabbis.

CHILD THREE: He was meek and smiling. And he loved kids!

CHILD FOUR: We took palm-tree branches and kept waving, and He waved back to us!

(They leave their palms under the cross and join the chorus.)

(LONGINUS, the Roman centurion, enters from the side, walking toward the cross. When he arrives, he takes off his hat.)

BARABBAS: Master Longinus, you remember me? After the revolution I caused, you were the one who arrested me. You were there under the cross. You saw when they freed me and took Him *(points to the cross)*. He must be a greater criminal than me, right?

LONGINUS: Barabbas, if I would have seen you any time before, I would have killed you. When the Jews asked to free you, I hated Pilate; I hated the Jews and hated you, too! But something happened. I don't like killing, and I don't hate anymore. Under the cross, I saw marvels and wonders. I have seen hundreds of people near death—scared, angry, and accusatory. He was different! He was calm. He said, "Father, forgive them." He forgave me, and I was one of His crucifiers. Above all, I believed in Him when I pierced His side. I had to. I was told to do it, actually. You see, we had to kill them all before sundown. We broke the others' legs, but he was dead, so I pierced his side. Normally nothing comes out from the dead, but I was soaked by the blood and water that poured from His side. He gave me life through His death. I screamed, "My Lord and my God." He is the living Lord.

BARABBAS: So do I deserve the freedom? Or was His cross mine?

LONGINUS: My place under His cross made me understand. Stay near the cross, and you will also understand.

(JOHN the Beloved enters from another side.)

BARABBAS: John, you are the beloved disciple. You have seen your master more than anyone. Is He more righteous than all? Is He really the Lord? Why did He take my place if He is God?

JOHN: He loved me! I had a place next to His heart. I heard Him saying, "One of you will betray Me." He washed my feet, and I couldn't help Him on the cross.

BARABBAS: You were the closest to Him, and you know Him the best. Why did He free me? He could have let me be crucified. What does He need of me?

JOHN: Everything He does is done for a purpose. Once He made us walk miles to meet a Samaritan. He has given you His life by taking your place!

BARABBAS: How? I am losing my mind!
JOHN: When I stayed next to His cross, He gave me His mother to be my mother. Barabbas, He would take your place and mine anytime.
BARABBAS: So I should stay under his cross?
JOHN: His cross or yours? What matters is that you stay near the cross, and you will understand.

(SAINT MARY enters. MARY runs to greet SAINT MARY and kisses her hands. Then they both walked to the cross. SAINT MARY kisses the cross and then steps away.)

BARABBAS: My Lord and my God. I was condemned, and You cleared me. I was cursed, and You honored me. I was imprisoned, and You freed me. I was sentenced, and You replaced me. I was dead, and You raised me.
MARY: Barabbas, this is Jesus's mother.
BARABBAS: Lady, I am very sorry. *(He kneels down, trying to kiss her feet.)* You must hate me. *(SAINT MARY touches his shoulder in kindness.)* They crucified Your son in exchange for me. I am sure that was very painful. I really do not know what to say.
SAINT MARY: Barabbas, it was not just pain. It was a sword that pierced my heart. Since He was born, I knew that the cross has its hour. That cross was before His eyes His entire life. They pierced my heart with Him, and mine bled like His. Barabbas, my son, my Lord took your place. For you and me, He came. He came for you and for every Barabbas *(points to everyone)*, every sinner, anywhere!

Barabbas, He is risen. Truly, He is risen! I did not have to go to the tomb like the others. I was sure He was going to resurrect. He wanted everyone to see His empty tomb, so they may believe. Barabbas, He defeated even death for you and every Barabbas here. He raised us all with Him, so we can all rejoice in Heaven with Him. Barabbas, rejoice! He took your death and gave His resurrection. Barabbas, go and tell everyone. He who did not spare His own Son but gave Him up for us all—how will He not also grant us everything? He IS risen! Truly He is risen!

(All proceed toward the cross, with BARABBAS in front of the cross. They all come one after the other, carrying the cross horizontally.)

BARABBAS: *(Kneels down.)* My Lord, You are my redeemer! How can I live Barabbas's life anymore? Barabbas also died on that cross—at the same time that you died for me. It is not I who lives but You who live in me. The life that I now have is not mine but Yours who loved me and gave Yourself for me. You are risen. Truly You are risen!

(The actors pick up the cross, with SAINT MARY in front and MARY at the back. DIMAS is on the right side, and BARABBAS is on the left. PETER, NICODEMUS, and the CHILDREN all stand behind SAINT MARY.)

ABOUT THE AUTHOR

Dr. Hani Ashamalla, clinical professor, Weill Cornell Medicine; radiation oncologist; and deacon, Saint Mary and Saint Antonios Coptic Orthodox Church, Queens, New York, was ordained as a deacon very early in life and considers the Coptic Orthodox Church to be like another mother. In addition to serving as a deacon, he is a supervisor for Sunday schools for high school students.

Raised in Egypt, Ashamalla earned a bachelor's degree in medicine in 1983 and a master's degree in chest diseases in 1986.

After immigrating to the United States in 1989, Ashamalla studied to become a radiation oncologist. He worked as an attending at New York Methodist Hospital, where he eventually rose to the position of chair of the Radiation Oncology Department in 2010.

Made in the USA
Columbia, SC
27 November 2017